Contents

List of Illustrations

Acknowledgements: Grateful acknowledgement is made to the following for their permission to reproduce copyright pictorial material: Gulbenkian Museum of Oriental Art, Durham (Fig. 1); Jacques Arthaud, Paris (Figs 2, 98–102, 104); the Estate of the late David McCutchion (Figs 3, 5, 8, 12, 14, 16, 33, 35, 36, 39, 47, 50, 57, 71); Jeffery Gorbeck (Figs 4, 6, 11, 22, 31, 37, 42, 46, 49, 75, 76, 77, 78, 79, 106); Koninklijk Instituut voor de Tropen, Amsterdam (Figs 7, 92, 95); Robert Skelton (Figs 9, 15, 18, 52, 60, 61, 63); Mark Hobart (Figs 10, 96, 97); Wim Swaan (Fig. 13); John Marr (Figs 17, 86); Garry Martin (Figs 19, 21, 23, 24, 25, 26, 27, 38, 41, 53, 59, 67, 72, 74); Office du Livre, Fribourg (Figs 20, 28, 32, 85 from Andreas Volwahsen, *Living Architecture: Indian,* Macdonald, London; Hennessey, Los Angeles, 1969); American Institute of Indian Studies, Varanasi (Figs 29, 31, 65, 66, 73, 81, 83, 87, 89); John Burton-Page (Figs 30, 58, 69, 84); Penguin Books Ltd (Figs 34, 43, 64, 93, 103—the last two with scale added—from Benjamin Rowland, *The Art and Architecture of India,* Penguin, 1953, pp 121, 178, 235, 268, 187 (Figs 14, 27, 42, 49, 29), Copyright © Benjamin Rowland, 1953; the Director of the India Office Library and Records, London (Figs 44, 51, 54); Alex Wodak (Figs 55, 56, 70); Ellen Smart (Fig. 62); Alfred Gregory (Fig. 68); Michaela Soar (Figs 80, 82); Federico Borromeo, Milan (Figs 88, 91, 94).

Principal Hindu temple sites of India and South-East Asia

3000 BC Harrapan culture
1500 " Aryan Invasion
6th cent. BC. Buddhism & Jainism
3rd/2nd BC. selecting deity Vishnu or Shiva

CHAMPA
Mi Son
Dong Duong
Angkor
Koulen
Roluos
Sambor
Prei Kuk
CAMBODIA
Po Nagar
Hoa Lai
JAVA
BALI
Singasari
Dieng
Kidal
Prambanan
Panataran

Preface

When I first wrote *The Hindu Temple* I conceived the book as a general introduction to a subject which was usually dismissed as 'exotic' or obscure. More than a decade has passed, and an increasing number of Westerners have travelled to India, Nepal and Bali and seen for themselves the temples; conversely, more and more Indian Hindus themselves have settled in Europe and North America and built their own shrines there. Scholars, too, have been active during this period, and numerous works have been published ranging from studies on Hindu cults and practices to detailed descriptions of particular monuments. As a result, I can no longer claim that Hindu temples are as unfamiliar to Westerners as they may have been a short time ago.

Yet there continues to be a need for a broadly based introduction to the subject which assumes no previous knowledge on the part of the reader, so the University of Chicago Press has decided to reissue this volume. While it was not possible for me to revise the text—which is reproduced here exactly as it appeared in the first edition—a few minor corrections have been inserted, several pictures replaced, and the Further Reading section brought up to date. On another occasion I might consider rewriting *The Hindu Temple* so as to incorporate my new historical perspectives and architectural information as well as that of other scholars, but I fully realise that this would result in a completely different work. Travellers and students evidently found the original book worthwhile, so much so that it became unavailable in three continents soon after publication. This indicates to me that the volume had been successful in fulfilling its original aim: to explain to the general reader something of the forms of Hindu temples and their sculptures, as well as to present the context in which these temples came to be built. I can only hope that this new printing will prove equally useful, and I am grateful to the University of Chicago Press for encouraging me to reissue the work.

As with any introduction to a complex subject it has often been necessary to present information in a simplified form, and generalizations have had to be made in order to encompass the multilayered nature of Indian civilization. In contrast, a detailed treatment has been found essential for the descriptions of particular examples of architecture, mythology and art. It is hoped that the reader will forgive the occasional abrupt transition from generalization to detailed description.

The book is divided into two parts: the first is devoted to aspects of Hinduism that are considered constant characteristics, while the second deals with factors of change, especially the development of Hindu sacred architecture and its art. Part One, "The Meaning of the Temple", presents information generally removed from any specific place or period, and applies to most parts of the Hindu world over the span of two thousand years. Here are described those features of Indian culture, partly defined by such terms as 'religion', 'mythology' and 'philosophy', which are but parts of the all-embracing worldview that lies at the core of Hinduism. Part Two, "The Forms of the Temple", concentrates on actual examples of buildings arranged according to considerations of geography and chronology. Both technical and stylistic aspects of sacred architecture are dealt with here, and the evolution of the Hindu temple is traced in some detail.

G. M., 1988

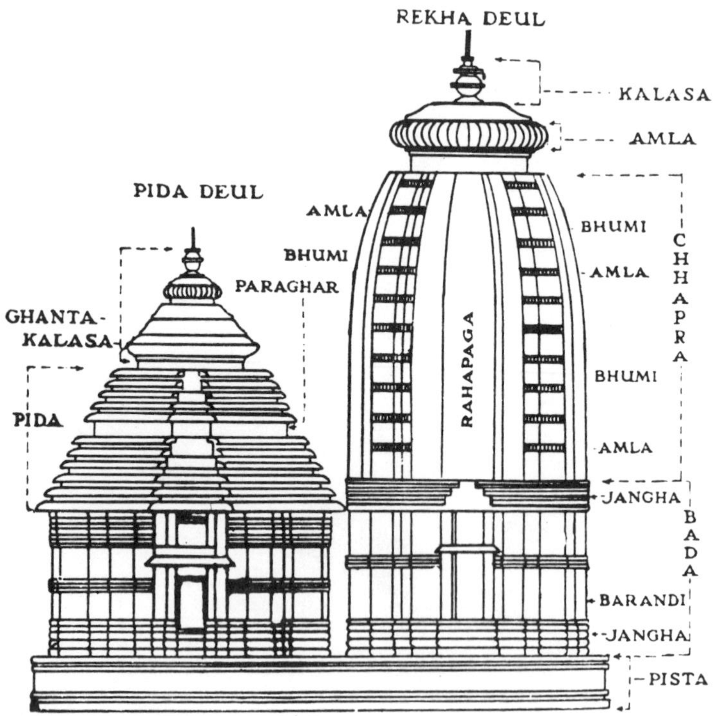

Elevation of a typical Orissan temple with the local terminology indicated

PART ONE
The Meaning of the Temple

1 The Civilization of Hinduism

For over two thousand years much of Asia has been dominated by Indian Hinduism as a religious, social and political force. Hindu Asia encompasses the subcontinent of India, the peripheral sub-Himalayan valleys, the major part of mainland South-East Asia and the Indonesian archipelago. However, the influence of Buddhism and Islam has also been pervasive in these areas during this period, and today only India, Nepal and Bali are predominantly Hindu, even though the whole region still retains vestiges of Hindu culture.

The temple is the most characteristic artistic expression of Hinduism, providing a focus for both the social and spiritual life of the community it serves. Temples have been built in all parts of Hindu Asia at different periods and continue to be erected in those countries which are still Hindu. The temple reflects the ideals and way of life of those who built it and for whom it was intended to operate as a link between the world of man and that of the gods. In order to understand the architectural forms and sacred art of the Hindu temple it is necessary to investigate the origins and development of the civilization that produced it.

The term 'Hinduism' incorporates a larger part of Indian civilization than is communicated by the word 'religion': it is a synthesis of many different beliefs and practices, modes of living and thinking. These differences are bound together by a cultural continuity and cohesive force that characterize Indian civilization. It is significant that nowhere in the extensive vocabulary of the Indian languages is there a word that corresponds to the term 'religion'—in fact, religious and non-religious matters are never distinguished in Hinduism as it is unimaginable that any activity, impulse or process can be without some divine potential. Hinduism spans the complete spectrum of Indian culture from the everyday agricultural life of the village to the transcendental speculations of the philosopher. At its most rarefied and abstract level, Hindu thought dismisses the world as illusory; it aims at breaking through this illusion to discover an ultimate reality beyond. The temple reflects this range of Hinduism and is much more than a mere setting for the practices associated with certain beliefs; it is imbued with a complex system of symbolism by which it embodies the most elevated notions of Hindu philosophy while still serving the requirements of everyday religious life. It is, therefore, an expression both of Hindu society and of the most profound levels of Hindu civilization.

The origins of Hinduism

Cultural contrasts are implied by the geographical features of the Indian subcontinent. The river plains of northern India are divided by hills from peninsular India with its raised plateaux and rocky outcrops. There are also variations in climate—the western regions of India, for example, are desert, in striking contrast to the eastern and southern extremities which lie well within the tropical zone. Though isolated from the rest of Asia by a chain of mountains to the north and by oceans on three sides, India has experienced at all times cultural influences from invading peoples who entered the country, mostly from the north-west. In fact, the origins of Hinduism may be understood as a reconciliation of the cultures of indigenous Indian populations with succeeding invaders. India fused these contrasting languages, beliefs and social patterns into the composite and conservative civilization of Hinduism.

The religion which is identified by the term 'Hinduism' did not appear until the centuries immediately preceding the Christian era. Its origins and earlier phases, however, introduce a further thousand years, and more, of Indian civilization. The literary tradition of Sanskrit, the sacred language of Hinduism, extends back to the middle of the second millennium BC when India was invaded by waves of Aryan peoples. The Aryans brought with them a distinctive language and religion which were closely related to those that appeared in Iran and, more remotely, to those of the Aegean and eastern Europe at about the same time, having been brought there by other Indo-European speaking invaders. Though these peoples were wanderers they were able to preserve some of their early traditions, which they later set down in a body of sacred writings, the Vedas. The religion that is contained in the Vedas is not to be identified with Hinduism, even though the Vedas are still regarded as the source for later sacred Hindu literature. The *Rig-Veda* is the oldest of these texts and was composed between 1500 and 900 BC in an early form of Sanskrit. Its 1,028 hymns were intended to be used at the sacrifices performed by priests in order to secure boons from the gods. The pantheon of deities described in the Vedas is dominated by powerful male gods mostly associated with the heavens. The greatest Vedic deity is Indra who fulfils the dual function of war-god and weather-god. The *Rig-Veda* used a subtle system of symbolism so that in later Indian thought its meaning was always open to interpretation at several levels.

Indian archaeology extends the chronological perspective back into the shadowy centuries of the third millennium BC, well before the coming of the Aryans. At this time there existed a remarkable civilization which flourished at sites along the Indus river and its tributaries. These are customarily grouped together under the title of Indus civilization, or 'Harappan culture', after the name of the first site at which this civilization was discovered. Excavations have revealed evidence of a highly organized culture concentrated in at least two large cities with regular street layouts and brick structures. Despite the fact that the buildings discovered cannot definitely be connected with any religious or ceremonial function, artefacts from these sites provide clues as to the possible beliefs of their inhabitants—cult figurines, especially 'goddesses', as well as seals and models of animals have been found in abundance. Some of the characteristics that are found in Hinduism after the Aryans arrived may be traced back to these river city cultures—for example, the worship of the female principle both as a maternal creative force and as an erotic and potentially destructive energy, the concern for the preservation of life including that of certain animals, and the cult of particular trees and plants. Other objects known from all periods of Indian civilization which are also found at these Indus valley sites include emblems of the male and female sexual parts, thus indicating the antiquity of the celebration of fertility in both male and female form.

The development of Hinduism

Over the centuries following the invasion of northern India by Aryan peoples in the middle of the second millennium BC, a distinct culture evolved, some strands of which bear little relation to the religion of the Vedas. These cultural manifestations may probably be traced to pre-Aryan beginnings—that is, indigenous to India—and may be tentatively identified with what is known of the Harappan culture. There are suggestions that by the time of the compilation of the *Rig-Veda* the Aryans had already absorbed many elements of the ideology of the civilization that they had found flourishing in the Indus valley. As the nomadic Aryan peoples settled down in the plains of northern India they gathered together in rural communities, some of which in time became urban settlements. Changes in living patterns were accompanied by changes in religion and the texts that were composed in the centuries following the Vedas, such as the Brahmanas and Upanishads, reveal the growing power of the priests who imbued the mystery of the sacrifice with a cosmic significance. From the pantheon of the Vedas the creator became more and more emphasized as a single divinity or godhead. In the Upanishads this godhead is further identified with the *atman*, the 'self' or spirit, which is formless but all-powerful and ever-present. A reaction to the prosperity of life is introduced for the first time in the cult of the ascetic individual who denies the enjoyment of life. The world of the senses is dismissed as unreal and the chief purpose of living is to secure an escape from a temporal existence. The notion of escape or release (*moksha*) from the present world underlies the beginnings of the doctrine of transmigration (*samsara*), in which the soul of man returns to earth after death in an endless cycle of rebirths. An important part of this doctrine is the concept of *karma* in which the actions of a human being in one life-span directly affect the rebirth that is to follow. It is in this context that Buddhism and Jainism appear in the sixth century BC. Neither of these two religious movements was originally concerned with an ultimate divinity; rather, they proposed ethical philosophies of everyday life which were directed towards the transcendence of human existence. This they combined with a concentration upon the lives and teachings of actual personages, who came to be worshipped as divine in later centuries.

By the third and second centuries BC, from the varied strands of the different cultures of the Indian subcontinent there had begun to emerge the new religion of devotional theism: thus begins the true history of Hinduism. The new religion reached its final form by combining influences from both the north and south of India and probably also from the cultures of other invading peoples who continued to enter India from the north-west during this period. The outstanding feature of the new Hinduism is the worship of a personal deity who generally took the form of a particular god or goddess, especially Vishnu or Shiva. The adoration of such a deity was believed certain to bring about the fulfilment of all the desires of the worshipper, even ultimate emancipation from the cycle of rebirths. The deities upon whom this new religion concentrated were basically syncretistic creations, having their mixed origins in the earlier pantheon of the Vedas and in various folk heroes, often regional gods or goddesses, of whom there is little record in early Indian literature. Before the beginnings of the Christian era the major cults of Hinduism had emerged which were to dominate the beliefs and practices of Hindus for the next two thousand years. At the same time, a host of minor divinities and spirits appeared who were no less important for human affairs. Elaborate rituals and ceremonies were rapidly evolved for the worship of these divinities, and myths and popular legends flourished.

During this period an enormous body of sacred literature was produced. The Vedas, Brahmanas and Upanishads continued to be regarded as the most sacred of India's religious texts and were studied by priests and theologians, as they still are today. However, the scriptures of popular Hinduism, available to all and not just to the priests, were the Epics, the Puranas or 'Ancient Stories', the books of Sacred Law and numerous devotional hymns. As these were not set down in writing until long after their composition, the period to which they originally belong cannot be determined with any accuracy. Even so, many of these texts may tentatively be dated to the early Christian era. The Epics express one aspect of the characteristic features of the new religion—the richness of contrasting cultural traditions. The *Mahabharata* and *Ramayana* were originally secular stories but at an early stage, probably before the Christian era, they developed a distinct religious character. The most celebrated portion of the Epics is the *Bhagavad Gita* in the *Mahabharata*, which is universally held to be a definitive statement of devotional Hinduism. The Puranas represent an even more popular aspect of Hinduism. They are compendia of legends and religious instruction which, in their present form, are not very ancient—none preceding the fourth or fifth centuries AD—even though they incorporate material that is very much older. A whole class of popular reciters of the Puranas grew up, travelling from village to village and commenting in the vernacular languages on their Sanskrit recitations. The religious hymns and poetry of Hinduism express much of the devotional theistic feeling that was popular in these early phases of Hinduism. In all of these texts the earlier pantheon of the

Vedas is overshadowed by a new repertoire of popular cults which were spread by such dissertations. Many of these folk cults concentrate on aspects of fertility which curiously contrast with the ascetic tendencies in the religion. The impact of Jainism and Buddhism is also of importance in the formative phases of Hinduism.

The emergence of the new religion and culture of Hinduism was soon to have its response in a sacred architecture and art, strongly influenced by the monumental architectural and artistic traditions first developed in India under Buddhist and Jain patronage in the second and first centuries BC. That earlier structures were fashioned from less durable materials such as timber, brick and plaster, means that the beginnings of Hindu architecture and art have either disappeared or are detectable only by the most fragmentary remains. It was not until the period of Gupta rule in northern India, from the fourth century AD onwards, that complete architectural schemes in stone were devised as settings for Hindu theistic cults. From the period following the Guptas, the building of temples in permanent materials for Hindu cults became a constant feature of Indian civilization. Patterns of history in India are characterized by a general lack of unification and continuous shifts in political and economic power; in addition, northern and southern India have had relatively independent histories. Since stone and brick architecture was mostly undertaken as a result of royal patronage, any account of the development of the Hindu temple and its art inevitably follows that of dynastic history. In the north of India the evolution of Hindu temple architecture was largely interrupted by Muslim invaders whose presence was increasingly felt from the eleventh century AD onwards, and many of the finest temples must have been destroyed. In contrast, the south of India was not to experience Muslim rule until a much later period, when it had a less disrupting effect upon Hindu traditions. Temple architecture in the south was therefore able to preserve a relatively unbroken development which has continued to the present day.

The spread of Hinduism

The dispersal of Hinduism to the kingdoms of mainland South-East Asia and the Indonesian archipelago was bound up with a more generalized expansion of Indian culture. In this process the religions of Hinduism and Buddhism, together with their theological systems and elaborate mythologies, the Sanskrit language and social system, came to be dispersed well beyond the confines of the subcontinent. Early contacts between India and other parts of Asia are traced back to the centuries immediately preceding the Christian era, and by the fourth and fifth centuries AD 'greater India' was already in existence. The means by which Hinduism spread beyond India is largely undocumented, but is most likely to have been stimulated by the priests accompanying merchant adventurers who probably set off on their colonial expeditions from ports on the eastern coast of India.

The great kingdoms that came to be established in South-East Asia were outwardly Indian in their culture and religion but, not surprisingly, the Hinduism that was fostered in these civilizations was a mixture of indigenous elements and imported Indian features. Among the most important notions incorporated into Hinduism outside India are those concerned with the worship of the ruler on earth as divine. The cult of the god-king (*devaraja*) never truly gained popularity in India but was of the utmost importance for cultural life and sacred architecture in 'greater India'. This cult was accompanied by a concern for the worship of ancestors and burial. Sacred architecture, therefore, developed a memorial and mortuary character. The Indianized kingdoms of South-East Asia experienced alternating phases of Hinduism and Buddhism, frequently combining them into one complex religious system. In the Himalayas, too, a mixed religious culture was fostered in which the erection of Hindu and Buddhist temples was sometimes carried out at one and the same time.

2 The World of the Gods

A great pantheon of gods, goddesses, semi-divine beings and lesser deities unfolds in the countless myths of Hinduism which exist in numerous versions throughout Indian literature, particularly in the Puranas and Epics. These myths present the collective wisdom of a timeless, anonymous and many-sided civilization and are much more than just fanciful 'biographies' of the gods. Like the great philosophical systems of India, the myths of Hinduism reveal the ultimate reality of the universe by giving symbolic expression to that which cannot be discursively expressed.

The gods are never far away from man. The elements of the landscape throughout Hindu Asia—the trees, hills, mountain slopes, caves, rivers, springs and lakes—are all imbued with a potential sanctity. Rudimentary markings in the landscape, such as a coloured paintstroke, a flag or pile of stones, indicate man's awareness of the proximity of the gods. In the Hindu temple the potentially divine becomes visibly manifest and therefore approachable by man. Sacred images in Hinduism are never mere effigies; their function is to make visible the world of truth. Since truth lies beyond the world of appearance, these images do not always conform to the evidence of human senses. The source of this art lies in the spectrum of gods vividly described in the enormous repertoire of Hindu myths and legends.

Time and the universe

The activities of the gods and the lives of human beings are linked together in a continuum in which time is conceived as a cyclical system. According to the Indian view the universe is destroyed by fire and is dissolved into the cosmic ocean out of which a new universe is created and another cosmic era begins. A single cycle of creation to destruction is sometimes described as one day of Brahma, the active creator-god of the universe. On the human time-scale, the blinking of an eyelid of the god Vishnu may encompass a complete life-span. In this manner mythology expresses the chronological sequences by which the divine and human time-scales are related. Each cycle of creation to destruction is divided into four ages (*yugas*) arranged in order of declining strength, peace and happiness. This inherent tendency towards destruction influences the affairs of both the gods and man. As man is mostly unable to perceive the cyclic nature of time and the universe, he can discover no explanation for the recurring rebirths that he must endure. His past, present and future lives are all linked together in a continuous time system, as are the actions of the gods and the dynamic mechanism of the universe. Man's entanglement in this cycle is likened to a spell or illusion (*maya*) and it is the aim of all Indian thought to learn the secret of this *maya* and, if possible, to cut through it into a reality that lies beyond. In Hinduism this liberating process is evocatively termed 'release' (*moksha*). The gods have compassion for mankind and when provoked by exceptional circumstances may reveal the delusion from which man suffers, thus indicating for him the path towards true knowledge.

Related to the time continuum of Hinduism is a spatial continuum in which an infinite series of universes is imagined, each isolated from the other and suspended in empty space. This conception of the cosmos is characterized by the shape of the universe, which is described as the 'egg of Brahma' (*Brahmanda*). This cosmic egg is divided into zones or regions, one of which represents the abode of human beings. Above are the heavens and beneath are the nether worlds. This model of the universe is related to Hindu

1 Diagram of the universe showing the 'rose-apple tree continent' (*jambudvipa*) with the oceans, continents and rivers arranged around the central mountain, Meru. Painting on cloth, western India, seventeenth century

astronomy and contrasts with another model which postulates a flat and circular universe. The centre of this latter scheme is the cosmic mountain Meru about which the sun, moon and stars revolve. Concentrically arranged around the base of Meru are the continents and oceans. The continent to the south upon which human beings dwell has a rose-apple tree as its distinctive flora and is known, therefore, as the 'rose-apple tree continent', *jambudvipa* (Fig. 1). This theologically determined cosmic model is of great importance for the Hindu temple, especially in the functioning of the temple as a symbolic reconstruction of the universe.

The gods and demons

Parallel to the recurring cycles of cosmic creation and dissolution is the concept of light and darkness as personified in Hinduism by the gods and 'anti-gods' (*asuras*) or demons. The complex themes of Hindu mythology are dominated throughout by the continuous enactment of light versus darkness,

2 The myth of the churning of the ocean: the gods pulling the serpent Shesha. Balustrade from the entrance to Angkor Thom, Cambodia, thirteenth century

good opposed to evil. Time never operates in a linear manner and the struggle is eternal; neither good nor evil can triumph for long. Though the gods are always fighting the demons and other powerfully opposed forces, they are also related in some way to their darker counterparts. So too are creation and destruction part of a single process. The very dynamics of the cosmos are expressed in the tensions of the conflict between good and evil rather than in an ultimate resolution which never takes place.

One celebrated myth in Hinduism vividly illustrates the interaction between the gods and demons—this is the churning of the cosmic ocean by means of the serpent Shesha who conveniently wrapped himself around the mountain Meru which, for this purpose, was supported on the shell of Vishnu who had assumed the form of a tortoise. The demons and gods took opposite ends of the cosmic serpent, the gods the head and the demons the tail, and by alternating pulling and pushing movements a churning action was set up by which the ocean was 'milked'. Eventually all that exists in the universe was produced, including the much sought after elixir of eternity (*soma*). In the Khmer monuments at Angkor this myth of search, struggle and creation is translated into a unique architectural feature—many of the temples are surrounded by a stone balustrade which is fashioned into the scaled body of a serpent, appropriately gripped by the gods and demons (Fig. 2).

The major cults of Hinduism

Innumerable gods and goddesses are found throughout the mythology and art of Hinduism, but the history of this religion at its highest devotional level is mostly bound up with the simultaneous development of two major cults—those of the male gods Shiva and Vishnu. A third cult is also of importance—that of the Mother or the Goddess—but is rarely seen in isolation, as the Goddess is essentially the consort of Shiva. These cults are synthetic in character owing to their evolution as amalgamations of many different minor deities. Shiva, Vishnu and the Goddess are compound creations with a wide range of divine powers and richly paradoxical personalities. The majority of Hindus ally their beliefs with one or other of these cults, worshipping Shiva, Vishnu, or the Goddess as the highest principle. In devoting themselves to one of these three deities Hindus do not deny the existence of the other two, who are regarded as minor expressions of the divine power. Thus in the cult of Shiva, Vishnu is considered an unimportant aspect, whereas in the cult of Vishnu, Shiva is reduced to a secondary emanation. To the worshipper of the Goddess, the male gods are mostly passive and shadowy figures.

In general, the cults of Hinduism developed peacefully together and only rarely is there any evidence of friction or religious persecution. The reason for this mutual co-existence is to be found in the belief that the ultimate godhead lies beyond the divisions of cult and that the worship of Shiva, Vishnu or the Goddess leads inevitably to the same goal. From this point of

3 Shiva *linga* in worship. The circular shaft of the *linga* is draped in cloth and stands upon an elevated circular pedestal identified with the *yoni* of the Goddess. A projecting spout carries away the libations of clarified butter and milk. Flowers and a Shiva trident are also in evidence

view the cult deities are all aspects of the divine in different forms. Such an attitude is responsible for the unusual degree of tolerance manifested throughout the history of Hinduism, and it has stimulated attempts to harmonize the cults. Shiva and Vishnu are sometimes worshipped together and the Goddess is also worshipped in conjunction with Shiva. There is also the concept of a triad of gods in which the minor deity, Brahma, is incorporated. Here, Brahma is considered to be the creator, Vishnu the preserver, and Shiva the destroyer. However, this celestial trio is only occasionally afforded significance in Hinduism.

Shiva

In its developed form the popular Hindu conception of Shiva arose out of the commingling of many cults. Despite these mixed origins Shiva is believed by his devotees to be the Great Lord (Maheshvara), the Greatest of the Gods (Mahadeva) and the supreme principle of the universe. The origins of the worship of Shiva are to be found in a pre-Aryan fertility god and in a fierce but minor deity of the Vedas called Rudra. In Hinduism Shiva is worshipped for his essential characteristic of energy, which is taken to be a direct expression of the inner workings of the universe. This energy dominates the many aspects and mythological appearances of the god; it may appear in the guise of fertility or as a force of destruction, and it is even inwardly directed in order to achieve the powerful meditation that characterizes the god in his ascetic role. The duality of sexuality and asceticism is everywhere found in the personality of the god Shiva.

Shiva is worshipped in the form of an erect phallus called *linga*, literally 'mark' or 'sign', which expresses the creative energy of the god (Fig. 3). Stone phallic emblems have been found in India from the earliest times and in Hinduism the cult of phallicism achieves a profound theological significance linked with this particular deity. Shiva is also worshipped as the Lord of the Animals (Pashupati) and his 'vehicle' (*vahana*) is the bull Nandi. In his destructive aspect the god directs his energy outwards, annihilating various demons and the enemies of his worshippers. Shiva is the god of the battlefield, the cremation grounds and the inauspicious crossroads, where he

4 The dance of creation-destruction; Shiva tramples the malignant dwarf. The god is accompanied by his wife Parvati and the bull Nandi. Ceiling panel from the Papanatha temple, Pattadakal, eighth century

is accompanied by ghosts, evil spirits, dwarf-like imps (*ganas*), and dogs. It is in this form that Shiva is known as Terrible (Bhairava), the destroyer of forces that threaten the well-being of the gods and man. No less characteristic of the god is his role as the originator and exponent of the various artistic accomplishments. Thus, Shiva is the Lord of the Dance (Nataraja) pacing out the cosmic steps of destruction-creation, the most vivid symbolic expression of his energy (Fig. 4). In contrast, Shiva is also the ascetic god seated among the peaks of his sacred mountain Kailasa, his divine energy directed inwards as he meditates upon the nature of the universe. He is the lord of mental and physical discipline (*yoga*), all knowledge and in particular the explanation of the sacred texts. His consort is the daughter of the mountain, the goddess Parvati or Uma.

Vishnu

To those Hindus who worship Vishnu this god is the embodiment of the source of the universe in which the qualities of mercy and goodness display themselves as an all-pervading force. Vishnu is responsible for preserving the balance between the natural order and disruptive powers of the universe. He is also ultimately responsible for the creation of the universe, the maintenance of order, and final destruction. According to a celebrated cosmic myth Vishnu sleeps in the primeval ocean upon the thousand-headed serpent Shesha dreaming the scheme of the universe (Fig. 5). From out of his navel a lotus stalk emerges, opening into a flower to reveal the seated god Brahma, the deity actually concerned with the task of creation. The cult of Vishnu owes its inception to a monotheistic devotional movement which promoted the notion of a composite god appearing in a number of different emanations and incarnations. Vishnu combines the man-god Vasudeva-Krishna with the creator-god Narayana from Vedic theology. Vishnu rides on Garuda, the eagle, and his consort is known variously as Prosperity (Shri) and Good Fortune (Lakshmi).

The doctrine of incarnations forms an important part of the cult of Vishnu. The term 'descent' (*avatara*) is here applied to Vishnu's appearance on earth in the form of a man or animal, or a combination of both, to further the act of creation and to preserve the well-being of mankind. As Hinduism developed, the number of incarnations came to be fixed at ten, even though certain incarnations tended to be more popular at different periods and in different regions of Hindu Asia. The first three incarnations of fish, tortoise and boar present Vishnu as the hero of myths concerned with the creation of the earth and its rescue from floods in times of crisis.

5 *Right* Vishnu sleeps on the cosmic serpent Shesha. Above are the gods Karttikeya on the peacock, Indra on the elephant, Brahma on the lotus and Shiva and Parvati on the bull. Beneath stand the five Pandava brothers, heroes of the *Mahabharata*, together with their common wife Draupadi. Dashavatara temple, Deogarh, sixth century

Vishnu as the tortoise supports the axial mountain Meru in the myth of the churning of the cosmic ocean. As the boar Vishnu raises the earth, personified by the goddess Bhumi, from the clutches of the serpent demon who had held her captive at the bottom of the ocean (Fig. 6). With the development of the cult of Vishnu other incarnations were assimilated such as the man-lion in which Vishnu appears in a revengeful and terrific form, and the dwarf

6 Vishnu as the boar rescues the goddess Bhumi from the clutches of the serpent demon. Cave-temple, Aihole, seventh century

7 Rama and Sita, chief characters from the *Ramayana*. Relief from the Shiva temple at Prambanan, Java, ninth century

incarnation of Vedic origin in which the god transforms himself into the pacer of the universe in three gigantic strides (Trivikrama). In the following three incarnations of Parashurama, Rama and Krishna, Vishnu comes to live among men as a warrior prince. Rama is the hero of the great epic, the *Ramayana*, and frequently appears with his beloved wife Sita and other characters from the story. Thus are introduced his brother Lakshmana, the monkey-accomplice hero Hanuman, and Ravana, the wicked seducer of Sita (Fig. 7). Krishna, around whom such a vast mass of legends is gathered, is the charioteer of Arjuna, one of the five Pandava brothers and the hero of the other great Hindu epic, the *Mahabharata*. In this guise Krishna delivers the celebrated sermon of the *Bhagavad Gita*, one of the most beautifully composed and popular religious texts of Hinduism. He is also the child-god, the youthful lover of the cowgirls (*gopis*) and the wise ruler. The cycle of

Krishna's boyhood deeds is among the most charming stories in Indian literature; the child-god is depicted engaging in domestic mischief while suppressing the activities of demons. As the young cowherd, the pastoral and erotic character of Krishna is stressed and his dalliances with the beautiful Radha (Fig. 14) form the subject of much romantic poetry. The last two incarnations of Vishnu, the Buddha and Kalkin, are probably later additions. The inclusion of the Buddha was originally intended to discredit Buddhists by depicting them as the victims of a false form of Vishnu created to delude demons. As Kalkin, Vishnu appears as a man riding a horse, heralding the destruction of the present era.

The Goddess

As in Europe, the worship of the female principle in Asia may be traced back to a very remote past, and a cult of the Goddess may have existed among the pre-Aryan peoples in India. In fact, a series of 'ringstones' have been found from the early periods of Indian history, representing the female counterpart (*yoni*) of the phallic emblem. During later stages of Indian civilization these objects came to be worshipped in themselves and are associated with magic diagrams (*yantras*) in the cult of the Great Mother (Mahadevi) who is sometimes identified with Parvati. In Hinduism the

8 The goddess Durga fights the buffalo-headed demon. She rides a lion and is assisted by warrior-like imps (*ganas*). Mahishamardini cave-temple, Mahabalipuram, seventh century

Goddess is considered the embodiment of the strength of the male god and, as such, is described as Energy (Shakti). She is the mother of all, embodying the child-bearing, nourishing and maternal principles, and is connected with the life-giving waters and lotus flowers. The variety of names and alternative forms that the Goddess assumes in Hinduism indicates her complex nature. The idea of the Goddess as the creative energy of the male god causes her to be associated with Shiva, with whom she develops some of her most characteristic features. The eternal couple Shiva-Shakti is represented by the conjunction of the male and female sexual emblems, the *linga* and the *yoni* (Fig. 3). According to a certain corpus of myths the Goddess is also the combined energies of all the gods, who created her and equipped her with their weapons so that she might destroy the buffalo demon whose power was mightier than that of the gods. In this forceful and destructive role, as Durga riding a lion or tiger, the Goddess pursues evil throughout the cosmos (Fig. 8). As the embodiment of the negative principle she becomes the fearful Chamunda and Kali, symbolizing the power of death, and in these forms she is sometimes considered the presiding deity of famine and disease. In her peaceful aspect as Parvati, Gauri or Uma, the Goddess is worshipped as the consort of Shiva, personifying the passive, benevolent and philosophical nature of her lord. Also of importance in the cult of the Goddess is her multiple appearance as a group of seven or eight Mothers (Matrikas), the personified energies of the major Hindu gods.

Certain sects of Hindus who worship the Goddess as the ultimate principle of the universe are known as Tantric after their scriptures, the Tantras. The followers of these texts believe that liberation is more effectively approached by following unorthodox means of religious observance. The Tantric sects break many of the conventions of Hinduism and indulge in sexual intercourse as part of their religious rituals. Magic diagrams (*yantras*) and verbal formulas (*mantras*) are utilized and class distinctions abolished at Tantric ceremonies. Associated with the worship of the Goddess in her Tantric aspect is the ritual slaughter of animals, especially goats, whose blood is offered to the Goddess in an attempt to appease her anger.

Minor deities

Other than Shiva, Vishnu and the Goddess, a number of other deities also receive worship in Hinduism, but only rarely do they emerge as independent cults. Perhaps the only god who approaches the popularity of the major cults is Surya, the sun. From the time of the Vedas the sun was worshipped in India as the supreme soul, the creator of the universe and the source of all life. Surya rides a chariot which is drawn across the sky by horses under the guidance of Dawn (Aruna). Related to the worship of the sun is that of the nine 'planets' (Navagrahas) which, in Indian astronomy, include the sun and moon (Chandra) as well as Mars, Mercury, Jupiter, Venus and Saturn. The planets play an important role in Hindu life as they form the basis upon which horoscopes are cast. The moon god is identified with *soma*, the essence

9 Nymph (*yakshi*) grasping a tree together with child attendant. Gauri temple, Bhubaneshwar, ninth century

of life, and with the beverage of immortality (*amrita*).

Sometimes connected with the act of creating the universe, Brahma is an important Hindu god. However, as an independent cult Brahma rarely gained popularity and is mostly subservient to the other gods, for whom he performs the various procedures of the Vedic sacrifice and other necessary rites. A significant minor cult is that of the guardians of the eight directions of space (*dikpalas*) in which important Vedic deities are incorporated, though reduced to somewhat minor roles: here are found Indra, Agni, Varuna (Fig. 15) and Yama. Also occasionally worshipped is the eternally youthful and chaste battle-god, the head of the celestial armies, known in different parts of India as the Leaper (Skanda), the Youth (Kumara), Karttikeya and Subrahmanya. Some confusion surrounds the birth of this god, who is believed to have grown from Shiva's seed that missed Parvati and which, according to different myths, fell into the fire, into the Ganges, or was fostered by the six stars of the Pleiades (Krittikas).

Folk deities

The panorama of gods and goddesses of Hinduism extends well beyond the deities of the major cults. A flourishing folk religion with a repertoire of demi-gods and spirits forms a large part of Hinduism. Almost no demarcation exists between the major cult divinities, more or less consistent in their character, and the more localized folk cults, varying from one region of Hindu Asia to another. In fact, the major cults of Hinduism themselves incorporate many of these minor folk deities who make only a limited appearance in the Sanskrit literature of Hinduism. It is interesting to learn that the oldest monumental sacred sculptures that have been preserved, such as those from central India dating back to the second and first centuries BC, do not represent the principal gods and goddesses of Hinduism but these folk spirits.

Even though Hindus regularly invoke the aid and favour of the major cult gods and goddesses, these divinities are beyond manipulation and can only be led in exceptional circumstances to comply with the requests of man. This means that the daily concern of many Hindus is with the worship of minor divinities whose special business it is to regulate matters of personal interest for mankind. Chief among these are the *yakshas* and their king, Kubera. These creatures are associated with fertility and prosperity and guard the riches of the earth; they are the protective divinities of the Hindu household and play a considerable role in local folklore throughout Hindu Asia. The *yakshas* are particularly important as guardians and gate-keepers (*dvarapalas*), in which roles they are provided with clubs and other weapons to expel unwanted visitors and evil forces. Related to the *yakshas* are the mischievous and playful imps (*ganas*) whose lord, Ganesha or Ganapati, is believed to be the son of Shiva and Parvati according to certain myths. Ganesha is of great importance to Hindus because he is the remover of all obstacles. His invocation is considered essential at the commencement of any undertaking such as building a house, writing a book, performing a dance or song and also at marriage ceremonies. The elephant head and rat 'vehicle' of Ganesha function as symbols of the god's ability to overcome obstacles both large and small.

Yakshis and *apsarases* comprise another important category of folk deities: these are the auspicious females associated with animals, trees and sacred waters. As an aspect of fertility, the *yakshi* often appears as a beautiful female embracing a tree which she gently kicks, a gesture deriving from a ritual of fecundation in which girls or young women impart their fertility to the tree (Fig. 9). *Yakshis* are mostly connected with a particular animal or with male companions, the *yakshas*, with whom they engage in amorous embraces. The *apsarases* are water nymphs, the courtesans and dancers of heaven where they entertain the gods. They are the perfect dispensers of sensual delights and erotic bliss (Fig. 10). In the personification of the two most holy rivers of India, the Ganges and Jumna, the goddesses Ganga and Yamuna embody health and abundance (Fig. 29). In common with these

10 *Left* Detail of heavenly courtesan or *apsaras* from Angkor Vat, Cambodia, twelfth century
11 *Above* Ceiling panel in the form of a coiled serpent with a human face. Cave-temple, Badami, sixth century

rivers the goddesses are able to purify all things. The Ganges is heavenly in origin and was brought down to earth, hence her purifying nature. Ganga sometimes appears in the mythology of Shiva where, according to certain stories, she winds around his sacred mountain residence, Kailasa, and through his matted hair in her descent earthwards. Another important deity is Shri or Lakshmi, the goddess of beauty and fortune, who is sometimes considered the consort of Vishnu but who is also independently worshipped for her own powers to confer prosperity and abundance. Her identification with the lotus flower betrays her aquatic origins, and she is born from the generative life-giving forces and riches of the waters of the immortal ocean. The goddess of knowledge and art, Sarasvati, is also of aquatic origin and is occasionally related to the god Brahma. She is the patroness of speech, song and wisdom. The role of music and dance is not to be underestimated in the religious life of Hinduism, and celestial choristers, musicians and dancers —the *gandharvas* and *kinnaras*—figure prominently among the minor divinities.

Serpents (*nagas*) have always been worshipped in Hindu Asia. Dwelling in the underground recesses, they are believed to be the keepers of the life energy that is stored in springs, wells and pools; they bestow prosperity and fertility, heal sickness and grant wishes. As such they are held in great awe and veneration (Fig. 11). Shesha, the king of the serpents, plays a part in the mythology of Vishnu and supports the god in his sleep upon the ocean (Fig. 5). There are also the guardians of the fields (*kshetrapalas*), who are important agricultural deities essential to the economic welfare of the village.

The gods in art

Hindu art is primarily an art of sacred images in which the gods, goddesses, demons and innumerable semi-divine beings take visible form. These sacred images draw upon human as well as animal and bird forms which are frequently mixed together in order to create composite creatures. Of great significance for Hindu art is the belief that outer forms can be assumed at will by the gods and goddesses, in order to aid the defective imagination of their worshippers who may otherwise be unable to perform the rituals of devotion. Divinity expressed as a transient form is a fundamental proposition of Hinduism and is reflected in its mythology and sacred images. For art, this means that the same deity is depicted in a number of different ways which may be employed simultaneously to suggest the various aspects of the god. The major divinities appear in a whole range of aspects and emanations, no one of which can usually be singled out as uniquely characteristic, for these multiple forms express the range of roles and powers of the divinity. The explanation of the origin of these multiple appearances is to be found in the syncretistic evolution of the Hindu cults. The art of Hinduism responds to this multiplicity; it is an art of countless sacred images, which communicates the different aspects of the divine while reminding the worshipper that ultimate truth lies beyond the world of appearances. Hindu art is dedicated to rendering the world of the gods visible; its sacred images voice the messages of the gods.

Figural art

The human figure is the source of inspiration for many of the images of gods and goddesses in Hindu art. So that these images may communicate the superhuman qualities of divinities, Hindu art frequently adopts the device of multiplying the heads and arms of its figures. Mythology often provides explanations for these departures from human anatomy—thus, the four heads of Brahma were created so that the god could gaze incestuously from different directions upon his daughter. Shiva, Vishnu and the Goddess are mostly provided with four or more arms (Figs 4, 5), and these multiple features are also employed for the images of many other deities. Whenever a god takes a 'human' form, such as Vishnu's incarnation as Rama (Fig. 7), these duplicate heads and arms are often abandoned. Human forms are also preferred for the images of a whole host of secondary and minor divinities in which deformities of the figure are sometimes employed to create grotesque images.

Sacred images of gods and goddesses are required to be beautiful so that they may persuade the deities to inhabit their outer forms. Hindu art has evolved particular physical types for its sacred images. For the gods, the shoulders and chest are broad, the waist slim, the stomach slightly overflowing the belt, the limbs solid and rather cylindrical (Fig. 5). For the female an elaborate headdress and jewellery, heavy spherical breasts, narrow waist, ample hips and a graceful posture are essential features (Fig. 10). Hindu figural art displays only sketchy attempts to portray such details of physical anatomy as musculature; rather, it is a quality of inwardly held breath that is conveyed. This breath (*prana*) is identified with the essence of life, the control of which is the object of religious discipline. The images of the gods and goddesses in Hindu art mostly have their bodies tautly drawn, as if containing a pressure from within.

Standing figures with their hands displayed in various gestures constitute an important category among the sacred images of Hindu art. There are also numerous examples of seated images in lotus posture (*padmasana*) with the soles of the feet turned up, or with one or both legs down. Images with more than four arms have these outstretched in a variety of postures. Important for standing images is the inflexion given to the posture by tilting the axis of the body; the favourite posture employs three bends (*tribhanga*) at the neck, shoulders and hips and is considered particularly appropriate for accessory figures. By contrast, the principal cult figures are mostly static in their postures. Almost all the gods and goddesses are depicted as standing or seated upon animal mounts. There are, however, a few images showing divinities reclining; these include the celebrated icon of Vishnu on Shesha (Fig. 5) and an image of the Goddess as a mother accompanied by a child. When depicted in episodes from myths images have more varied postures, especially if they are engaged in acts of destruction or hunting. Provocative postures, expressive of an undisguised sexuality, are present throughout Hindu figural art, particularly in the depiction of female deities. There are also important contacts between figural art and sacred dance which are well illustrated in the images of Shiva pacing out the steps of creation-destruction (Fig. 4) or performing his victory dance upon the prostrate body of his opponent.

One of the most distinctive characteristics of Hindu figural art is the significance accorded to the gestures of the hands (*mudras*). It was in Buddhist art that the importance of hand gestures was first realized and this practice continued in the Hindu artistic tradition. The positions of the fingers and thumbs of the hands of sacred images are expressive of the characters of the gods and goddesses in both their benign and fearsome aspects. The uplifted outward-facing palm bestows grace upon the worshipper (Fig. 4), while the downward palm signifies submission. These and many more gestures are employed throughout Hindu figural art. Like the different postures of the body these gestures also relate to dance, where every hand and body movement is imbued with meaning to create a language of motion by which the sacred myths and stories are communicated.

Facial expression on the images of Hindu divinities is mostly inward-looking, detached and other-worldly; only occasionally do cult images express the fleeting momentary glances of human beings. This calm expression is sometimes retained when the deities are engaged in violent pursuits, curiously contrasting with the energetic posture of the body (Fig. 8). However, fearsome facial expressions are also utilized in Hindu art for the portrayal of the terrific aspects of gods and goddesses. Here the eyes protrude in a demonic stare, the mouth has fangs and the tongue drips blood, illustrating the constant flux of destructive forces. In the majority of sacred images a consistent facial type is retained which has survived numerous stylistic variations. In goddesses the face is rather full with fish-shaped eyes, the eyebrows fashioned in the contour of an arched bow. The nose is sharply defined and the lips are full. The facial type for male deities is curiously similar, there being little distinction between male and female (Fig. 12).

The importance of emblems

Physical appearance is seldom employed in Hindu figural art as a means of distinguishing one deity from another, and identification mostly relies upon the recognition of the emblems held in the hands. These emblems symbolize the power and nature of the deity and as such have come to be worshipped as cult objects independent of the divine images to which they usually belong. In the cult of Shiva, the phallus (*linga*) indicates the procreative energy of the god and is mostly preferred to an image of the god for purposes of worship (Fig. 3). In his quasi-human form Shiva is provided with a series of characteristic weapons; in particular, the three-pronged trident (Fig. 4). In some of his aspects the god carries the half-skull begging bowl and noose typifying his terrific nature and connection with death. For Vishnu two emblems are imbued with a special significance; these are the conch and wheel-like discus, both used as weapons in war. The conch shell (Fig. 6) functions as a symbol of eternal space and the heavenly atmosphere. When blown it is supposed to produce the sound of the primeval waters. The wheel-discus represents eternal time and the power to destroy all things. For the Goddess as well as several other minor deities, a variety of effective weapons indicates the superhuman power of destruction (Fig. 8).

Variety and arrangement of emblems are important in the identification of the different aspects of the major deities. Accordingly, Vishnu has his emanations classified as twenty-four, the same number as the permutations by which two emblems and two *mudras* may be rotated between four arms. Among the more popular emblems in Hindu figural art are ritual instruments such as rosaries, ladles and water-pots; musical instruments, both stringed and percussive; objects expressive of female beauty such as flowers and mirrors; and an enormous range of weapons such as bows and arrows, swords, spears, clubs and banners. The association of divinities with war and hunting is most marked in Hinduism and reveals the tribal origins of some of these gods. There is little consistency in the appearance of emblems in the sacred images of Hinduism, and chronological and regional variations are considerable.

As emblems symbolize the nature and power of the god and goddess, there is found in Hindu art the rather curious habit of personifying these emblems so that they take on human features. In the cult of Vishnu, small figures occasionally appear holding the auspicious conch and discus. Some versions of the Shiva *linga* are provided with faces of the god symbolizing the divine energy radiating outwards. The 'face-*linga*' (*mukhalinga*) provides an excellent example of the intimate relation between figural and symbolic forms in Hindu art (Fig. 12).

Animals and birds in art

One of the special features in the depiction of Hindu divinities is the animal or bird 'vehicle' (*vahana*) that accompanies the deity. This vehicle is not only a means by which the god or goddess is transported; it symbolizes an

12 'Face-*linga*' from the Shiva temple, Bhumara, sixth century

essential aspect of the divine personality. Thus Nandi, the agricultural bull of Shiva, is fully expressive of the god's sexuality (Fig. 4) and the lion or tiger mount of Durga embodies her fierce strength and aggressive nature (Fig. 8). The river goddesses, Ganga and Yamuna, are identified by their accompanying mounts—the crocodile monster (*makara*) of the Ganges and the tortoise from the Jumna. Lakshmi is mostly found in conjunction with elephants which reinforce her association with water, lotus flowers and good fortune. Sarasvati is accompanied by the swan of pools and lakes (*saras*) which typifies her grace.

Animals and birds function also as a convenient means of distinguishing images from one another and there is an animal or bird appropriate for almost every god and goddess. Without their quasi-human counterparts, animals and birds are able to suggest the deity to whom they belong and are also worshipped beyond the connection with gods and goddesses. In fact, animals and birds have a life of their own in Hindu art. In a further expansion of the transience of forms that is assumed by divinities there exists in Hindu art a remarkable series of hybrid forms in which human, animal and bird features are combined: the sacred images of Hinduism abound with numerous human figures provided with animal heads (Fig. 13), or human heads with animal bodies. Multiplicity of features is also adopted by these hybrid creatures. The origins of sacred images in which human and animal components are combined may perhaps be sought in the tribal and totem-like religions of the non-Sanskrit cultures of Hindu Asia. Characteristically, Hindu mythology provides explanations which attempt to see these hybrid forms as essential to the personality of the deity. Thus the nature of the boar, which is equally at home in water or on land, is important for the boar incarnation of Vishnu (Fig. 6), and the terrific nature of the lion is said to explain the man-lion form that Vishnu assumed in order to devour a particular demon-king. Semi-divine beings and a whole range of mythological creatures are also hybrid. Paramount among the hybrid animals are the serpents (*nagas*) who appear in a variety of forms, their divine nature indicated by multiple cobra heads. Human and reptile aspects are sometimes combined most intimately—the serpent body appearing behind a human figure which is sheltered by a canopy of hoods (Fig. 11), or the reptile head joining a human torso in which sexual differences are shown. The mythological bird, Garuda, is the traditional enemy of the serpents and sometimes holds a pair of them in his eagle-like claws. Garuda is mostly depicted in a hybrid form with a human torso and bird beak, wings and claws. Other hybrid creatures also combine human and bird forms. Among these are the *kinnaras*, the celestial musicians, who appear as attendant figures throughout Hindu art. Their human bodies are provided with wings, bird-like feet and plumed tails; their human hands play musical instruments, especially those with strings.

13 *Right* Kneeling guardian figure with monkey head. Banteay Srei temple, Angkor, Cambodia, tenth century

Sacred images

Representations of the major cult deities form a large part of Hindu art. The depiction of Shiva varies with his different aspects but certain common features permit an easy identification of the god. Shiva's hair is long, matted and mostly piled up; it is sometimes decorated with a small skull, a figure of the Goddess Ganga and the crescent moon. The ears are sometimes dissimilar, one being long and pendulous with a large earring hanging from it. A third eye is often placed vertically in the centre of the forehead. The god usually has four or more arms whose hands carry a variety of weapons and emblems. Those by which the god is best known are the trident, drum and small deer. Shiva is decked with snakes which serve him as scarves, bracelets and belts, and he is also ornamented with jewellery. The god appears dressed in the skins of the animals that he has killed, such as the tiger and elephant, and he tramples a writhing dwarf, symbolic of cosmic ignorance (Fig. 4). In his terrific aspect Shiva is depicted with protruding eyes and fangs, his innumerable arms brandishing a fearful selection of weapons. He is garlanded with skulls and holds a half-skull begging bowl. In an unusual aspect as the Great Lord (Mahesha), Shiva has four heads, only three of which are sometimes visible.

Images of Vishnu depict the god with a high crown whose shape forms a tapering cylinder behind which a halo is often placed. His four or more arms carry a variety of weapons including the characteristic conch and wheel-like discus. In his different *avataras* the images of Vishnu greatly vary. As the fish and tortoise, Vishnu is either a hybrid creature with a human head attached to a fish or tortoise body, or a purely animal form. In images of the boar and man-lion, these figural and animal elements are usually reversed, the god having the head of a boar or lion upon a human body (Fig. 6). As the dwarf, Vishnu appears in art as a small figure carrying a parasol, the mark of a wandering ascetic. When transformed into the gigantic god of the cosmos, he is shown kicking one of his legs upwards as he takes the three strides which encompass the earth, sky and heavens. These last two forms of Vishnu are sometimes found combined within a single artistic composition. In his three 'human' incarnations Vishnu appears with only two arms, carrying the apparel of war appropriate to Parashurama, Rama and Krishna. Krishna is variously depicted—there are the playful scenes of the child-god, the young cowherd playing the flute who is the youthful lover (Fig. 14) and also the royal personage protecting mankind. As the Buddha, Vishnu is shown seated in the lotus posture with the characteristic Buddhist curled hair and topknot. As the incarnation of Kalkin the god rides upon a horse or, alternatively, has a horse head upon a human body. Sometimes the depictions of the *avataras* of Vishnu are combined into a single image: thus the god as the embodiment of the worlds, 'Form of All' (Vishvarupa), has up to four side-heads including the lion and boar indicating these incarnations.

An 'ideal' type of female beauty dominates many of the images of the

14 Krishna playing the flute accompanied by his consort Radha. Terracotta panel from the temple at Loada, Bengal, nineteenth century

Goddess, particularly in her benign aspect as Parvati, Gauri or Uma. Naturally, the Goddess is depicted in art as a beautiful young woman, usually with two or more arms; she has heavy breasts, a narrow waist and ample hips. She frequently holds a lotus flower in one of her hands. It is difficult to distinguish these forms of the Goddess from each other and Parvati, Gauri and Uma are only recognized from the context in which they appear. In her fearful role as Kali, Durga and Chamunda, the Goddess is easily distinguished. Like images of Shiva in his terrible aspect, those of the Goddess have innumerable arms each holding some deadly weapon including the spear and sword, whilst long and matted hair, protruding eyes, fangs dripping with blood, and garlands of skulls around withered breasts are all typical features.

Of great interest in Hindu art are the syncretistic images created as composite figures, the worship of which permits the devotee to apprehend two deities simultaneously. Harihara, in which Vishnu and Shiva are combined, is depicted as a male figure with four arms, two of which on one side carry emblems of Shiva, the other two having emblems appropriate to Vishnu. The vertical demarcation between the two gods is clearly visible in the headdress, where the piled hair of Shiva and the tapering crown of Vishnu merge. Another popular image is that of the androgyne (Ardhanarishvara) in which Shiva and Shakti are joined. Here a composite figure is created, one side of which is female, the other male. This image, therefore, presents the curious spectacle of only one breast with a single female hip and shoulder.

Surya, the sun god, rides a chariot drawn by seven horses under the direction of Aruna, the charioteer. In his early appearance in Indian art, Surya wears boots and a cloak, thus betraying his foreign artistic origins. He stands erect with only two arms which hold open lotus flowers; behind his head is a large disc representing the sun. Surya frequently appears in conjunction with the other 'planets' such as the moon, Chandra, who is recognized by the crescent outline placed behind his head. Images of Brahma, the creator god, are easily distinguished from those of the other deities (apart from Shiva in an unusual aspect) by his characteristic four heads, only three of which are visible in relief sculpture (Fig. 5). In his four hands Brahma holds various ritual objects such as rosary beads or the spoon and ladle by which he pours oblations onto the sacred fire; his vehicle is the goose. Images of the guardians of the eight directions of space are each identified by their different mounts and emblems. Indra, the guardian of the east, is accompanied by an elephant and holds a thunderbolt; Agni, regent of the south-east, is surrounded by flames and holds a water-pot; Yama is the guardian of the infernal regions which are located in the southern direction, he rides a buffalo and holds a club, a sign that he is the messenger of death; Nirriti overlooks the south-west and rides upon the shoulders of a man, holding a club; Varuna, the overlord of the terrestrial oceans and guardian of the west, is recognized by his noose (Fig. 15); Vayu, the personification of wind and regent of the north-west, holds a flag which flutters; the guardian of the north-east, Ishana, is depicted as an aspect of Shiva. Skanda, Kumara, Subrahmanya or Karttikeya, the many-titled and youthful battle god, appears in art with numerous arms which display weapons of war

15 *Right* Varuna, the god of the waters and guardian of the western direction. Rajarani temple, Bhubaneshwar, eleventh century

(Fig. 5). He is sometimes provided with six heads indicating his association with the six stars of the Pleiades who are sometimes regarded as his foster-mothers.

Images of the folk deities, the *yakshas*, are recognized by their pot-bellies; they usually hold clubs in their two or more hands, and their hair is mostly formed in small ringlets. Kubera, their king, carries a sack of treasure. *Yakshas* appear throughout Hindu art, particularly in their role as protective guardians. In this capacity they sometimes carry the emblems of the gods they guard—thus as Shiva door-keepers, they frequently hold tridents and snakes. Related to images of the *yakshas* are the pot-bellied *ganas*, or imps, who attend upon Shiva. Sometimes given heads of different animals, these imps are depicted in playful and sometimes obscene postures with sexual deformities; they also appear as musicians accompanying the dancing of Shiva (Fig. 4). Their king, Ganesha, is distinguished by his elephant head, and in his four or more hands holds a variety of emblems including a hatchet, a ball of rice, and a broken tusk. According to legend Ganesha broke off the tusk to hurl it at the moon who had laughed at him. Around his stomach is a belt of snakes.

Mythology and art

Hindu art provides numerous instances of the god and goddesses taking part in scenes from myth. Prominent among such scenes are those showing the deities slaying their enemies in violent and terrifying postures. Hindu art demonstrates great skill in choosing the most telling moments from the dramas in which each deity plays a dominant role. Shiva rides a chariot drawn by Brahma and shoots his arrows at the demons of the triple cities who have threatened the welfare of mankind; he thrusts his trident through the body of the blind demon; he dances victoriously within the outstretched skin of the elephant demon that he has just killed; and he paces out the cosmic steps of destruction-creation upon the back of a prostrate dwarf (Fig. 4). As the man-lion, Vishnu grapples in hand-to-hand combat with his enemy and also savagely rips open the demon's body in order to devour the entrails. Krishna subdues the serpent demon, Kaliya, by dancing upon his cobra hood, and the Goddess violently slays the buffalo demon with her sword. Other stories stress the miraculous appearances of divinities in order to rescue their devotees. Thus Shiva suddenly materializes in order to prevent the god of death, Yama, from claiming a staunch worshipper who has desperately clutched a *linga* that he has worshipped. Vishnu emerges from the ocean as the boar to rescue the earth goddess, Bhumi (Fig. 6), or descends upon Garuda to save an elephant trapped in the waters by the serpent demon; he also transforms himself from a dwarf into a giant who encompasses the universe. In all these stories the moment of rescue or miraculous manifestation is chosen for the depiction of the god in art.

Certain myths propound the superiority of one cult deity over another. Shiva appears within a gigantic fiery *linga* in order to prove to Vishnu and

16 Episodes from the *Ramayana*—the fight between the monkeys and Rama's enemies; the building of the bridge to the mythical island of Lanka. Kailasa temple, Ellora, eighth century

Brahma that he is the supreme principle of the universe. In the illustration of this myth the boar and goose, representing Vishnu and Brahma, are suitably overawed by the immeasurable dimensions of Shiva's *linga*. The Goddess owes her creation to the combined energies of the gods and she is frequently shown in artistic compositions as larger and more powerful than the deities on whose behalf she eventually slays the buffalo demon (Fig. 8). Stories of creation, especially associated with the mythology of Vishnu, are of great importance in art, such as that of Vishnu sleeping on the serpent

(Fig. 5) and, as the tortoise, supporting the axial mountain Meru in the churning of the ocean.

Also significant in Hindu art are the scenes of adoration in which cult images of divinities come to be worshipped. Such scenes often appear as the final episodes in the depiction of myths and are intended to indicate to the devotee the suitability of his pious acts. Thus in a temple dedicated to Shiva, worshippers may be depicted in attitudes of devotion before an image or symbol of the god, together with accessory deities and mythological beings.

Hindu art displays a preference for celestial 'family groups' in which the gods are shown together with their various consorts, children, attendant figures and animal or bird vehicles. Shiva and his consort Parvati, with Ganesha and Karttikeya who are often considered to be their children, are depicted in their mountain retreat of Kailasa. Nandi, Shiva's bull mount, *ganas* and ascetics are also in attendance. When the multi-headed Ravana threatens their peace he is rapidly subdued by the crushing pressure of Shiva's toe. In addition, there are compositions of the marriage of Shiva and Parvati in which Brahma acts as priest. Doubtless, such scenes reflect the desire to bring together into a single artistic composition many of the contrasting elements within a cult.

In order to illustrate the epic stories of the *Mahabharata*, *Ramayana* and various Krishna legends, Hindu art evolved a narrative series of successive scenes in which episodes from these stories are depicted. Particularly popular are the battle scenes from the *Mahabharata*, as well as episodes from the *Ramayana* in which Rama and his brother Lakshmana, and also the monkey-accomplice Hanuman, fight numerous demons and overcome extraordinary obstacles in their search for Sita, Rama's abducted wife (Fig. 16). The climax of the *Ramayana* is the fight between Rama and Ravana, the wicked king of the mythical island Lanka, who has imprisoned Sita. Krishna legends, too, are popular subjects for narrative art, especially the stories drawn from the childhood of the god and his youthful dalliances with the beautiful Radha.

3 The World of Man

From the Hindu point of view, the lives of human beings are merely stages in the progression towards ultimate liberation. The world of man is the sum total of countless individual life-spans bound up in the cycle of rebirth. Liberation is accessible to all human beings, though never within a single life-span. In the world of man the temple functions as a symbol of ultimate enlightenment: it is the house of the gods among men, the place where the gods may be approached and divine knowledge discovered. As the centre of religious and cultural activities, the temple is the focus of all aspects of the life of the community it serves. But the temple is also the product of a desire to transcend the world of man—the principles of its construction, the forms of its architecture and decoration, as well as the rituals that take place within its walls, are all aimed at ultimate liberation.

Hindu society is traditionally divided into a hierarchy of four principal classes, each with its own distinctive way of life and separate duties. Though there is a common law (*dharma*) for all to follow, there is also a law appropriate to each class and to each stage in the life of the individual. According to this theory, the highest of these four classes, the brahman, is considered divinity in human form. In Hindu society the brahman enjoys great privileges and from this class come the professional priests. At all times many brahmans led truly religious lives and members of this class constituted the theologians who set down their ideas and beliefs in the language described as 'perfected', Sanskrit. It is in this language and its derivatives that many of the sacred books of Hindu religion and philosophy are written. Some learned brahmans also came to hold high positions at royal courts, at which they were frequently influential in the affairs of state. From the *kshatriya* or warrior class came many of the rulers of the kingdoms of Hindu Asia, while the *vaishya* or mercantile class provided the guilds of artisans and craftsmen. As the patrons and the builders of temples these two classes had great importance for the development of sacred architecture. The lowest class, the *shudras*, acted as servants and labourers and had little relation with the temple. In some communities *shudras* were not admitted inside temple enclosures. Outside the Hindu social system were the 'untouchables'.

To the traditional Hindu the religious and the secular life are never truly distinguished, and the ordinary procedures of everyday life necessitate frequent contacts with the divine, whether it be with the 'high' cult deities or the lesser folk spirits. These contacts take place in the home, one room of which functions as a miniature temple with an image for worship, or at the local temple where priests officiate. For the three upper classes of Hindu society the temple is a place of both daily worship and occasional worship on a particular occasion; it may also be an object of pilgrimage at festival times. Every community in Hindu Asia, even the smallest village, has its place of worship, the temporary habitation of the gods. Differences in prosperity and in political and cultural importance between towns and villages account for much of the variety in the scale of temple architecture, the techniques of building and the particular deities that are worshipped there. Lack of historical information about many Hindu temples makes it difficult to distinguish these factors. Even though potent sites for temples are frequently dictated by sacred geographical features, which means that significant temples are sometimes located beyond the confines of towns and villages, Hindu temple architecture mostly forms part of an urban or village environment.

Royal patrons

The climate of Asia is not conducive to the preservation of historical records unless they were inscribed on stone slabs or metal plaques. Little information has survived about most Hindu temples and their builders, and in the case of smaller temples, perhaps built of mud or timber, it is unlikely that any such information was ever committed to writing. From the few records that have survived it is clear that temple building, at least in stone, was mainly carried out as a result of royal patronage. Stone construction involved much labour, time and organization, all of which was extremely expensive, and only rulers who had access to the concentrated economic wealth of a country could afford such building activity. That stone temples were costly undertakings is indicated by the number of cases in which the material itself is known to have been transported from a quarry far away from the temple site. Workmen with different skills had to be employed and organization and supervision of the building project maintained. Major craftsmen responsible for the design and execution of particular parts of the temple and priests to officiate at the various ceremonies were highly paid and had sometimes to be brought from another region.

Temple building seems to have been a sincere expression of the devotion and piety of the ruler. Hindu literature frequently describes the merit that is due to the patron of the temple. 'Let him who wishes to enter the worlds that are reached by meritorious deeds of piety and charity build a temple to the gods', suggests the *Brihatsamhita*, an early text, while the later *Shilpaprakasha*, a manuscript on temple building, ensures that the patron 'will always have peace, wealth, grain and sons'. The erection of a temple for the gods was also undertaken for the benefit of the whole community that it served, and whose common spiritual aspirations it embodied. In this way the ruler of a community provided his subjects with the facilities by which their spiritual life might be maintained. There was also the possibility of achieving fame, if not immortality, because 'everything vanishes with time, only a monument lasts forever', according to the *Shilpaprakasha*.

Temple building communicated the physical power of the ruler as it was an expression of his economic resources.

Inscriptions carved on the walls and columns of temples throughout Hindu Asia from many periods demonstrate that private individuals or groups of individuals were also able to function as patrons. There are numerous records of contributions of money, treasure or income towards the fashioning of a sculptural panel, the renovation or upkeep of a temple, or for the performance of certain rituals. Not all of these individuals belonged to the ruling classes; guilds of wealthy merchants played a particularly prominent part in the patronage of temple architecture. However, the role

17 Rajendra, the Chola ruler, receives a floral garland of victory from Shiva who is seated with his wife Parvati. Brihadeshvara temple, Gangaikondacholapuram, eleventh century

18 *Above* Gilded bronze image of Bhupatendra Malla, ruler of the Kathmandu valley. Durbar square, Bhadgaon, eighteenth century

19 *Below* Coronation scenes of the Pallava kings. Drawing of part of a relief from the courtyard of the Vaikunthaperumal temple, Kanchipuram, eighth century

of the royal patron, not only as financier but as co-ordinator and visionary in building projects, never diminished. As temples became larger, more elaborate and more costly, public subscriptions or additional taxes were sometimes introduced to provide a further source of revenue. The erection of ever larger temples as part of increasingly ambitious projects exerted a considerable strain upon the economy of a kingdom, and it seems that the power of some Hindu Asian dynasties declined at about the same time as their building activities reached maximum proportions.

Temple building was sometimes undertaken in celebration of an important political event. In the middle of the eighth century the two queens of the Chalukyan king Vikramaditya II built temples to Shiva at the royal site of Pattadakal to commemorate the victory of their husband over the neighbouring Pallava ruler (Fig. 75). In the early eleventh century the Chola king Rajendra extended his empire northwards and conquered the armies of the ruler of Bengal. To celebrate his march to the Ganges, Rajendra erected a temple to Shiva at his capital city Gangaikondacholapuram. In a niche beside one of the doorways of this temple is a relief carving depicting the god Shiva together with his consort Parvati; beneath, the king Rajendra receives a floral garland of victory from the god (Fig. 17). Portraits of the royal patrons of temples in the buildings themselves are rare in India. Temple architecture in Nepal sometimes incorporates commemorative stone columns, upon which an image of the ruler is placed facing the principal entrance to the temple (Fig. 18).

Scenes of royal coronations and honour form the subject of much temple art, thus providing evidence that rulers of kingdoms attempted to link their

lives with the world of the gods. In the eighth century temple at Kanchipuram dedicated to Vaikunthaperumal, an aspect of Vishnu, the interior walls of the colonnade around the courtyard are covered with carved panels. Here is found the whole history of the Pallava kings from which scholars have been able to reconstruct the dynastic chronology. Coronation scenes are particularly prominent (Fig. 19) and there are also many episodes of warfare. In fact, military campaigns form a popular subject of decoration throughout Hindu temple art, and illustrate connections between the lives of rulers and the building of temples. Elephants, horses, footmen and soldiers are all popular motifs.

More complex associations between kingship and temple building are found in the Hindu temples of Java and Cambodia. The ancient kings of these countries sometimes identified themselves with incarnations of the gods, upon whom the safety of the realm and success of the ruler depended. Here were evolved rituals and cults of the god-king (*devaraja*) centred upon the sacred *linga* which was imbued with the essence of divine kingship. According to these cults the temple was dedicated simultaneously to the god and the king himself. Angkor Vat in Cambodia, where the climax of Khmer temple architecture is to be seen, introduces a further variation upon this theme since it is also a temple of death. The complex forms of its architecture focus upon the central building dedicated to Vishnu which is also a sepulchre of its founder Suryavarman II who died in 1152 (Figs 103, 104). Reliefs carved on the gallery walls of this temple illustrate the mythology of Vishnu together with processional scenes from the life of the founder king. Yama, the god of death, also appears.

The artist and society

Traditional Hindu society makes no allowance for the individual pursuit of self-expression. The role of the Hindu artist is to give visible form to the values of his society, rather than to communicate a personal interpretation of these values. The artist is considered an instrument by which things higher and greater than himself find expression in the forms that he creates, whether these be works of architecture, painting or sculpture. The notion of signing a work of art is of little importance as it is believed that the artist does not himself directly imagine the work—he is 'guided' and functions only as the executor. For this reason most works of Hindu art and architecture are anonymous. That the artist thought of his work as a means of access to the divine is demonstrated in the large amount of literature that describes the mental preparation and ritual purification that he is to undergo before commencing the work. Only in this way can the artist identify himself with the transcendental principles to which he attempts to give visible form.

Of great importance for the evolution of Hindu art was the relationship that developed between artists and brahmans. In order that certain theological ideas should be translated into art, particularly in the fashioning of sacred images, the priests set out elaborate prescriptions which governed all the details. The earliest records of these prescriptions occur as sections in the Epics and Puranas; later they are found gathered together in the Shastras and Agamas. These texts on image-making reflect the ambition of theologians to codify all aspects of the production of sacred images in stone, metal or wood, and even painted images, and there is substantial evidence of the success of their efforts. The earliest periods of Hindu art, at least from the period of Gupta rule in the fourth century, were characterized by considerable freedom and variation in the images chosen to depict the divine. With the development of Hindu art, especially from the ninth and tenth centuries onwards, much of this freedom was lost and there was an increasing consistency in the choice of images and their appearance with regard to costume, posture and physique, and the emblems that the figures hold in their hands. The fuller and more naturalistic images from the earlier periods became stiffer and more stylized as Hindu art developed. The disciplines of iconography and iconometry were increasingly applied, presumably reflecting the influence of brahman theologians. As temple projects became larger, both in India and in other parts of Hindu Asia, there was an accompanying increase in the number of images that had to be fashioned in either stone or metal. The expansion of the production of Hindu art was accompanied by an increasing dependence of the artist upon the brahman for the suitable forms of sacred images. Even so, the essential role of the artist in society as giving expression to its values remained unaltered.

Craftsmen, guilds and the builders of temples

Among the few surviving records that describe the erection of temples is a remarkable palm-leaf manuscript recording in detail the building operations of the thirteenth-century Surya temple at Konarak in Orissa. The manuscript lists the workmen, their salaries and rules of conduct, and provides an account over several years of the various building operations. It has been possible, therefore, to reconstruct many of the economic and organizational procedures of this particular building project. Much of the information may be taken as typical of other temples both within India and in other parts of Hindu Asia.

The architects, artisans and workmen engaged in the various activities associated with the building of a temple were organized into groups which functioned as guilds. The traditions of these guilds were mostly preserved orally, the guilds being extensions of family units in which techniques were handed down from one generation to the next. As the means of livelihood of these families depended on their knowledge and skill, traditions and techniques were often jealously guarded. The guilds united both the family and the individual craftsmen into a single corporate body. They fixed rules of work and wages and set standard prices for work completed, and their regulations had the force of law. Over their own members guilds had judicial rights and could expel a rebellious member. They exercised control over the social life of their members, ordaining who could be married to

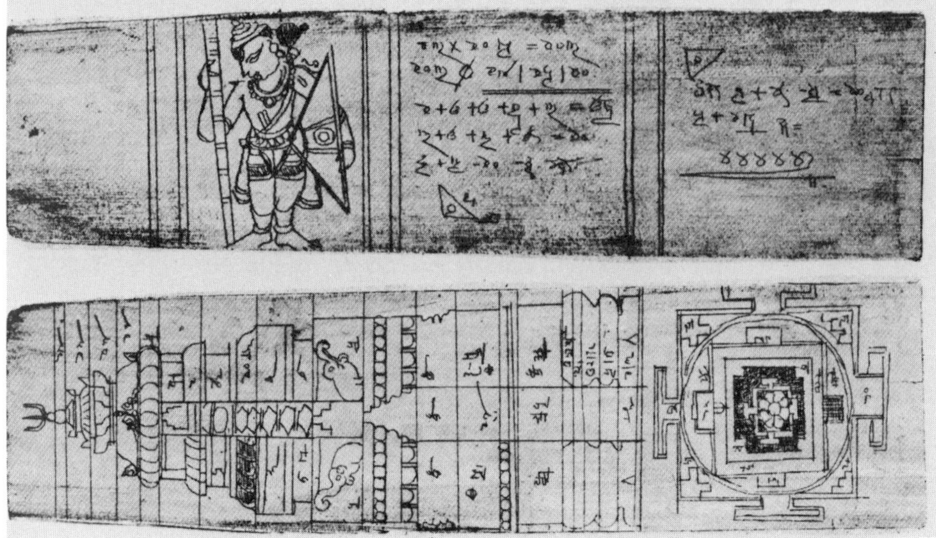

20 Two sides of a palm-leaf from a manuscript on temple building. *Above left*—the architect of the temple holds a surveyor's rod; *above right*—calculations of proportions; *below*—the vertical section of the temple is marked with height indications and rises upon the *mandala* regulating the temple plan. Orissa, seventeenth century

whom and even acting on occasions as guardians of widows and orphans. Guilds frequently became wealthy and powerful and there exist many inscriptions recording their charitable donations. That members of guilds frequently travelled from one region to another in order to work on different projects accounts for much of the spread of architectural and artistic traditions that took place throughout the history of the temple.

Most important among those involved in the erection of a temple were the chief architect (*sutradhara*) (Fig. 20) and the superintendent of works, almost his equal in authority. Also of importance were the head stonemason and the chief image-maker who co-ordinated those responsible for the architectural and sculptural portions of the buildings. Sculptors (*shilpins*) were engaged on all portions of buildings and, judging from the intimate connection between architecture and sculpture in Hindu temples, their services must have been required at many stages in the work. It would seem that many of these workmen comprised whole families, for whenever someone had an accident, fell ill or died, there was always a family relation to take his place. Women were also employed for lighter auxiliary work such as clearing and polishing stones. Workmen settled in camps around the building site; they had their meals in a common mess staffed by cooks, kitchen supervisors and servants. The building of the temple proceeded over most of the year, but during the rainy season when work was halted workmen were generally given leave. Holidays were celebrated when the royal patron came on a visit, when a son and heir was born to him, or when an important part of the building was completed. There were officials for the maintenance of law and order and administrators for settling any internal disputes. Fines were imposed as punishment for delay in delivering materials or completion of the work. Doctors were also present to look after the sick and injured. There were barbers, and men who served refreshments to the workmen engaged in fine chisel work, while another team of menials provided drinking water; there were also oilmen to feed the torches and lamps during work at night.

A crucial role in temple building was played by the learned brahmans who were expert in the theory of art and who had to give advice and guidance to the workmen whenever required. The brahmans performed various ceremonies at every important stage of work for the removal of obstacles or when some accident required atonement. There were also important consecrations such as the purification of the site, the initial tracing of the ground plan, the setting of the crowning finial of the superstructure, and the instalment of the principal image or symbol of the divinity in the sanctuary.

Architectural and sculptural work was assigned on the basis of contracts for separate operations, each contract probably having a different leader for each task. Payment of the workmen was related to these contracts. The chief architect and superintendent of works did not usually have contracts for any particular task; rather, they were responsible for co-ordinating the various stages of building and directing the entire project. There were workmen for every skill—stonemasons to cut stones to size, artisans to fashion them into architectural forms, and sculptors to do the finest chisel work (Fig. 21). Specialists carried out particular jobs such as laying out the axes of the building, marking out the plumb and square lines which regulated the carving, grinding the polishing materials, carving the bands of friezes and mixing the coloured pigments for paintwork. Leading master-craftsmen worked on the principal images of the sanctuary and its outer walls. Though the products of the great masters were probably executed with the assistance of other workmen, the design and composition of each panel were almost certainly the inspiration of a single artist.

21 Cutting, chiselling and transporting stone for temples. Sketch of a panel from Khajuraho, eleventh century

The temple as a focus of culture

The temple has always been the centre of the intellectual and artistic life of the Hindu community, functioning not only as a place of worship, but also as a nucleus around which all artistic activity is concentrated. To begin with, general education within the temple was of great importance, with the teaching of such subjects as grammar and astrology as well as the recital and teaching of sacred texts. Many endowments to temples were specifically made for the establishment of colleges which were incorporated into temple complexes. Apart from schools connected with temples, which mostly catered exclusively for brahman pupils, there also existed scope for popular education. The spacious halls of temples were settings for recitations of the Vedas, the Epics and Puranas, and the singing of hymns and devotional chanting, of benefit to the whole community. Music and dance generally formed part of the daily ritual of the temple and during special celebrations and annual festivals these played a particularly dominant role. Large temples would maintain their own musicians, both vocal and instrumental, together with dancers, actors and teachers of the performing arts.

In the patronage of architecture, sculpture and painting the temple has been of paramount significance throughout the history of Hindu civilization, and there can be little doubt that the greatest efforts in these were always directed towards sacred architectural projects. Despite the countless stone and brick temples of Hindu Asia from all periods, there are only exceptional instances of secular structures built in these materials.

The economy of the temple

Sources of wealth for the Hindu temple consisted mainly of donations from royal patrons and private individuals. These were received by the temple in the form of money, valuable objects, livestock or income from grants of land, including whole villages and their inhabitants. Donations might be made for a number of reasons, including gratitude for services rendered by the temple, or perhaps in fulfilment of a vow. Grants not only financed the building of temples but also provided for their upkeep and renovation. There were grants for the performance of rituals, perhaps in perpetuity for a certain individual. Donors were stimulated by the notion that a grant to a temple would promote religious merit and increase the possibility of their ultimate salvation. Substantial donations were likely to propagate the reputation of an individual or the power of a ruler. There was also the desire to record a pious act in the form of an inscription or to have a portrait of the donor made in sculpture or painting.

As grants accumulated, temples became wealthy and could afford to become employers and act as patrons. The wealth of a temple was usually invested in land and in this respect the temple came to function as a landlord. From the produce of the land came income upon which the economic life of the temple was based. Projects of cultivation and land reclamation were embarked upon, and in order to facilitate cultivation the land was usually leased to tenants. These leases, as indeed all economic transactions of the temple, were entered upon in the name of the god to whom the temple was dedicated. This served to emphasize the sacred character of the transaction, reminding the landed tenants that they only temporarily held sacred land. Usually strict and efficient control was exercised over the tenants and fixed units of measurement were established by which to measure the grain that was brought in. However, the tenants were protected by the temple and there are records of loans being made and credit extended to needy cultivators. The holders of temple land were permitted to enjoy a proportion of its produce and as this was a hereditary settlement, the land passed from one generation to another. Improvements in agriculture were also embarked upon by the temple, and sometimes there was the provision of such facilities as water tanks, canals and new roads. The lands belonging to the temple were mostly exempt from taxes.

Some temples enjoyed independent jurisdiction and also the right to prevent any kind of 'pollution' from the entry of undesirable persons into their locality. The area under temple control was considered sacrosanct and inviolable, and conferred immunity from military attack. In times of danger and political unrest temples would sometimes serve as fortresses protecting members of the community.

As temples provided work and the means of livelihood for a large number of persons, they were able to exert great influence upon the economic life of the community. Even small temples needed the services of priests, garland-makers and suppliers of clarified butter, milk and oil. The authorities of the temple entered into contracts with individuals or groups who undertook to supply specified goods and services at stated periods: clarified butter for burning lamps, the number vastly increasing with the ever-growing endowments of devotees, flowers for garlands, rice for offerings and for the feeding of brahmans, vegetables and fruits, sandal-paste and incense. Securities were demanded and penalties enforced on defaulters. One of the most detailed accounts that have been preserved of the number of people who were supported by a temple and the wages they received is that given in an inscription on the Brihadeshvara temple at Tanjore dating from 1011. The list includes dancing-girls, dancing masters, singers, pipers, drummers, lute-players, conch-blowers, superintendents of temple women and female musicians, accountants, sacred parasol bearers, lamp-lighters, sprinklers of water, potters, washermen, bearers, astrologers, tailors, jewel-stitchers, brazier-lighters, carpenters, and superintendents of goldsmiths, totalling more than six hundred persons. Most of the employees rendering these services were part-time as payment was in land which they had to cultivate. In return for the execution of the contract with the temple, the employee was entitled to live off the produce of the land. Some gratuitous services were usually considered obligatory, such as dragging the temple chariots on festival occasions and helping when a large building project was undertaken.

Among the employees of the temple were specially chosen and highly esteemed maidens (*devadasis*) whose services were dedicated to the god of the temple. These temple maidens played an important role in dancing as well as in the singing of devotional hymns by which the temple god was entertained; they also bore lamps for the deity. Girls were admitted to the temple before reaching puberty and after an appropriate period of training they were 'married' to the god by means of a special ceremony.

The temple has traditionally been foremost among charitable institutions in Hindu society. In records of gifts to temples the stipulation is often found: 'to provide for worship, for gifts of food to the assembly of ascetics and for repairs'. Generally wayfarers, whether pilgrims or other devotees, took their food in the temple together with many of the temple employees. The fare was by no means sparse and consisted of cooked foods, especially rice. On festival occasions the cooking might be most elaborate. Some temples would house a number of residential students in boarding schools attached to the temple. There are also instances of hospitals associated with temples in which beds were provided for the sick. The most important role of the temple in matters of charity was the feeding of brahmans on sacred occasions. Endowments frequently provided for the feeding of specific numbers of brahmans in temples after the offerings had been made to the gods. Sometimes feeding houses were established in which free food would be offered daily throughout the year. Feeding of the poor was also widespread, with cooked rice offered as a public charity to the poor of the lower classes.

4 The Temple as a Link between the Gods and Man

The Hindu temple is designed to bring about contact between man and the gods; it is here that the gods appear to man. The process by which this contact is made comprises a series of ideas and beliefs incorporating a complex symbolism. Dynamic rituals and ceremonies permit a realization of these ideas through which the Hindu temple functions as a place of transcendence, a place where man may progress from the world of illusion to knowledge and truth. The rituals and ceremonies that lie at the very core of the religious life of Hinduism, as well as the more elusive ideas and beliefs that accompany divine personages, have fundamentally influenced the forms of temple architecture. Some of the earliest records of these symbolic ideas and beliefs are found in the Epics and the Puranas; in later periods they form the subject of chapters in texts on sacred architecture such as the numerous Shastras and Agamas. These texts are often concerned with imbuing sacred architecture and its art with symbolic meaning and are the work of theologians who compiled them from many different sources.

The fundamental preoccupation of Hindu thought is with man's release (*moksha*) from an illusory world into which he is recurringly born. The architecture of the Hindu temple symbolically represents this quest by setting out to dissolve the boundaries between man and the divine. For this purpose certain notions are associated with the very forms and materials of the building. Paramount is the identification of the divinity with the fabric of the temple or, from another point of view, the identification of the form of the universe with that of the temple. Such an identification is achieved through the form and meaning of those architectural elements that are considered fundamental to the temple. Hence the significance attached to the site of the temple, its ground plan and vertical elevation and the dominating images of mountain, cave and cosmic axis. A sacred mathematics is created, composed of a language of precise measurements, which permits a symbolic realization of the underlying cosmic ideas. The relationship that develops between forms and their meanings within the Hindu temple is essential to its function as a link between the gods and man.

The temple as a house of god

The willingness of the gods and goddesses of Hinduism to make themselves visible and accessible to man is emphasized everywhere in Hindu literature. That temples are places where the gods make themselves visible is conveyed by the very terms used to designate a temple: a seat or platform of god (*prasada*), a house of god (*devagriham*), a residence of god (*devalaya*) or a waiting and abiding place (*mandiram*). The temple is a receptacle for the gods, who may appear there in the forms imagined by their worshippers. These forms are embodied in the sacred images or symbols of the deities which constitute the most important part of Hindu art.

Sacred images and symbols of the deity to whom the temple is dedicated are housed in a small sanctuary within the temple known as the 'womb-chamber' (*garbhagriha*), a term indicating that here is contained the kernel and essence of the temple. The sacred image or symbol of the god represents a means of union with the divine but is not usually identified with the deity—the god or goddess only temporarily resides within the fabric of the image. Such an occasional coincidence of form and divine presence only occurs after the sacred image or symbol has been prepared for worship by elaborate rituals of consecration and then ceremoniously enshrined. Precise laws regulate the production of these sacred images and symbols so that they may function successfully as suitable receptacles for the deity. The devotional cults which are served by the Hindu temple inevitably focus upon this sacred image or symbol of the deity in the 'womb-chamber', but devotion also extends to encompass the temple as a whole. Thus the temple is not only a place of worship but also an object of worship. The divinity that is revealed within the sanctuary may also be revealed in the very fabric of the temple itself. From this point of view the architectural and sculptural components of the temple are considered to be an evocation of the presence of the divine. To this end mythology, folklore and art meet in a common attempt to portray the varied manifestations and exploits of the gods and goddesses. All of Hindu art aims at recreating the celestial environment of the world of the gods.

As sacred images and symbols in Hindu art represent only temporary receptacles for the gods and goddesses who intermittently inhabit their outer forms, so the temple as a whole is also understood as a temporary abode of the gods in the world of man. In the temple the divine is always potential, but only on occasions is it manifested. Rituals and ceremonies are essential to promote this manifestation of the divine and, in fact, the priesthood of a temple is resident in order to maintain the continuous presence of the god. There are also the particular occasions when the community or an individual needs to approach the gods. If the necessary rituals are not performed, the temple lies dormant as the deities are not 'in residence'.

Rituals of temple worship

It is the direct worship of gods and goddesses (*devapuja*) that forms the focal point of the religious activities embraced by the Hindu temple. The various rituals of worship permit an identification of the worshipper and the place and means of worship with the godhead. Those who are able to achieve a unity of self and godhead through ritual gain merit and access to the path that leads to ultimate liberation. Practices of temple worship originated before the principal Hindu cults had become differentiated, and rituals performed in temples dedicated to the cults of different deities follow more or less a basic pattern. Worship is conceived as an evocation, reception and entertainment of the god or goddess as a royal guest, reflecting the ancient association of royalty with the divine. There is also the belief, which has been particularly popular outside India, that the ruler's power is an extension of the divine law. The practices of temple worship are strictly laid down in a series of texts devoted to ritual, some of which may be traced back to the Puranas and earlier. What may be observed of rituals and ceremonies in present-day Hindu Asia indicates that they have not basically altered from what was practised in the earliest periods of Hinduism, even though the ancient rituals have doubtless become greatly simplified.

Before ceremonies can begin the priests who are to perform the rituals must first be prepared. Bathing and other acts of purification are necessary in order to promote the transformation by which the priests are able to identify themselves with the divine object of worship. At the ceremony there is no need for a congregation to be present as rituals are performed by priests on behalf of the community. However, devotees who desire to benefit from the influence emanating from these rites may also be present. The absence of a congregation reveals the fundamental role of the temple priests, who represent the community they serve and who are responsible for its satisfactory relationship with the divine. Upon this depends the happiness, welfare and success of the members of the community.

Temple ritual for an ordinary day consists of four celebrations which take place at sunrise, noon, sunset and midnight. The ceremonies usually begin with the reverential opening of the door of the sanctuary, or 'womb-chamber', in which the image of the deity is housed. The powers guarding over the door are saluted, and there is the sounding of the bell and the clasping of hands before the sanctuary is entered, in order to expel any unwanted spirits and to attract the attention of the god or goddess. The priest then expresses his intention of worship and asks the divinity for consent. Hymns are recited to persuade the deity to take visible form by inhabiting the image or symbol and once this takes place the priest is able to converse with the divine. Various verbal formulae (*mantras*), sacred syllables (*bijas*) and symbolic hand gestures (*mudras*) are then employed to concentrate the power of the god or goddess and to permit the performer of the ritual to draw himself into contact with the divine. The worship proper consists of the awakening of the god or goddess, who is considered to be asleep when unmanifested. Due attention is paid to the comfort of the divine presence, the preparation of vessels and ingredients necessary for worship, the bathing and dressing of the sacred image, and the offering of refreshments. The image is anointed with oils, camphor and sandalwood, garlanded, and entertained with moving flames. The offerings which are next presented vary considerably but usually have cooked foods such as rice forming the principal meal of the god. Several circumambulations (*pradakshinas*) are then executed around the image where it is free-standing and the priest bows and offers a handful of flowers. Finally the sanctuary door is closed as the deity is again considered

to be asleep. In this manner a typical ceremony is completed, to be repeated at the other appropriate times of the day.

In addition to these daily ceremonies there are also opportunities for private worship in the temple by individuals who make offerings to the deity, recite prayers and perform suitable circumambulations. Such private worship usually takes place between the regular ceremonies when the god or goddess gives 'audience' to the priest. Private worship may be undertaken as the result of simple devotion, or for some particular reason, perhaps in the hope of securing divine assistance in a time of trouble, danger, pain or sickness. Vows and presentations of offerings by laymen are an important part of the activities in any Hindu temple. Ceremonies such as the investiture of the sacred thread for brahman boys which is the commencement of their religious life, marriages, and oaths for civil and criminal cases also take place in the temple, either in front of the sacred image of the sanctuary or in the temple compound. Devotees and other individuals who wish to approach the deity are first required to purify themselves by bathing. They then present their offerings to the priest who places them at the feet of the god and recites the appropriate sacred hymns and prayers.

Some forms of worship that take place in the temple are more congregational in character. For example, public performances of sacred song and dance to glorify the worshipped god or goddess are an important aspect of the activities of the temple, as are the recitals of ancient texts and their exegesis by learned priests. Other ceremonies occur at regular intervals and are sometimes treated as festivals. Every important temple throughout Hindu Asia has regular festivals which consist mainly of processions and enactments of particular myths and are sometimes most spectacular. Processions have a particular significance for the community because the sacred image or symbol from the sanctuary of the temple, or its substitute, is brought outside to become visible to those who may not generally be admitted into the temple. Devotees have the opportunity of directly presenting flowers, fruits and other offerings to the god or goddess who is carried in procession. The processional image is not always the same as that which is permanently housed in the sanctuary, but for the purposes of ceremony it is identified with that image. Great attention is lavished upon the chariot (*ratha*) on which the processional image is carried and which may be an elaborate structure of timber, bamboo and canvas. The chariot functions as a temporary and mobile temple throughout the festival (Fig. 22). Of particular significance in festivals is the link with the agricultural life of the region, and they often coincide with the planting or harvesting of a crop. Festivals provide opportunities for the mingling of mythology and folklore expressed in performances of music, dance and theatre as well as for the manufacture of temporary images of clay or earth for special ceremonies.

22 *Left* Mobile temple—the chariot bearing the processional image is pulled by villagers at a festival near Badami

Dynamics of the temple

Associated with temple festivals is the undertaking of pilgrimages to sacred places. In Hinduism the attainment of spiritual perfection is likened to a long journey of many stages, frequently visualized as a progression upwards through various stages of consciousness. Likewise, the temple is conceived as a place of transit, a ford or crossing-place (*tirtha*). In the rituals that take place within the temple the movement of the worshipper and priest is of greatest importance. There is the symbolism of the passage through the doorways which is connected with the idea of transition from the temporal to the eternal. But the most significant aspect of devotional dynamism in Hinduism is the circumambulation (*pradakshina*) which proceeds in a clockwise direction around a sacred person, image or object and even around the temple itself. This circumambulation is a rite constituting a bodily participation in movements and prayer. In some cases it is translated into architectural forms and many temples are furnished with ambulatory passageways. Circumambulation takes the worshipper from the doorway of the sanctuary, housing the image or symbol of the deity, around the sanctuary in a clockwise direction where further cult icons introduce other aspects of the divine (Fig. 23).

The centre of the sanctuary functions as the focus of other dynamics which are realized through a process of symbolic association. To begin with there is the radiation of energy outwards from the centre of the sanctuary in four directions. The sacredness of the image in the 'womb' of the temple expresses itself as a powerful force whose influence expands outwards: hence the potency of sacred images that are aligned with these forces, especially those positioned in the centres of the north, west and south sanctuary walls. These secondary images are often given prominence by being set within projecting and elaborately decorated niches. As a further extension of the idea of these lines of energy providing potency, images are placed at the four corners as well as at the centres of the sanctuary walls (Fig. 24). A connection with the guardian deities of the eight directions of the universe is sometimes realized in temple architecture with the positioning of the eight gods around

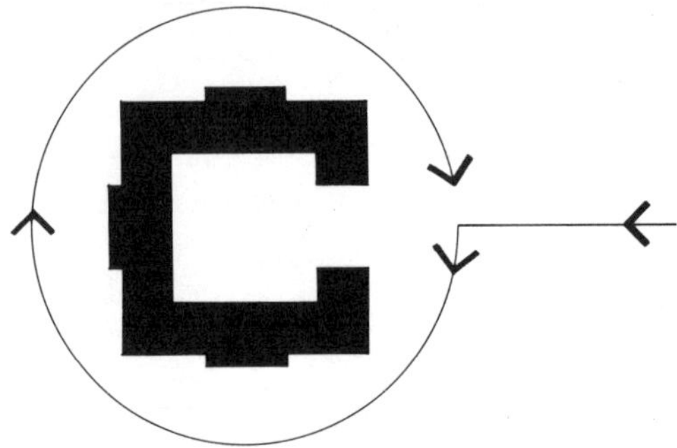

23 The dynamics of temple worship—the approach to the sanctuary and the circumambulation around it in a clockwise direction

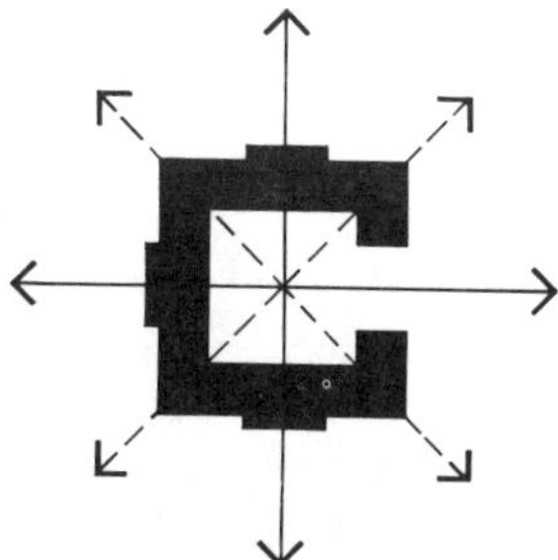

24 Outward radiation of energy from the centre of the sanctuary. Along these lines of energy are positioned important secondary images of the deity housed within the sanctuary

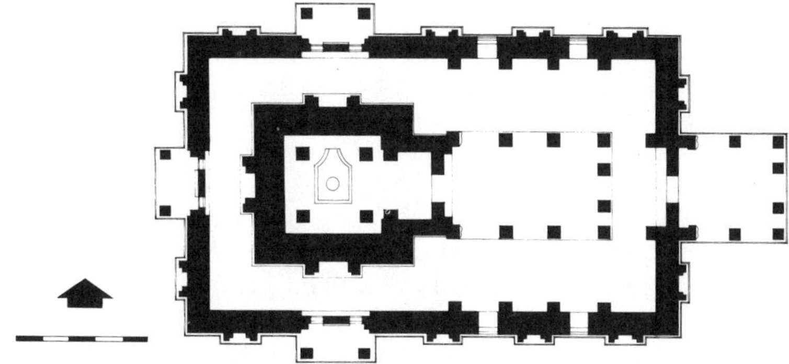

25 Plan of the Svarga Brahma temple, Alampur, seventh century. In the appropriate niches of the outer walls are positioned the *dikpalas*, the guardians of the eight directions of space, and two syncretistic deities *(here and throughout each scale division represents one metre, unless otherwise stated)*

the temple (Fig. 25). Penetration inwards towards the centre of the sanctuary, usually conducted along an east-west axis, is of the greatest importance in ritual for the worshipper, and this too has had its effect upon the development of temple architecture. The interior spaces of temples are arranged to promote the movement of the devotee from the outside towards the sanctuary through a series of enclosures which become increasingly sacred as the sanctuary is approached. At the final stage in the penetration towards the centre, when the doorway of the sanctuary is reached, the priests take over from the worshipper and conduct offerings to the image of the deity inside the sanctuary. This is undertaken on behalf of the worshipper who must wait outside but who follows the movements of the priests, accompanying their actions symbolically. A further expression of the energy of the sanctuary radiating outwards is in the movement upwards; though the worshipper cannot physically participate in this ascent, the symbolism attached to the parts of the temple permits him ritually to undertake such movement.

The Hindu temple serves as a reminder of impermanence, a notion that implies a turning away from the present illusory world in an effort to surmount and to transcend it. Though the temple with its art may be indispensable for the rituals of worship, it marks only a transitory stage in the journey from the temporal to the eternal. Mythology juxtaposes relative time sequences and cosmic eras as the keys to the inner mechanics of the universe. This overlapping of cycles of time and repetition of cosmic eras finds visual expression in the forms of the temple, where architectural and sculptural motifs repeatedly appear in different sizes in different parts of the building. The finial placed at the summit of the temple symbolizes the absolute and timeless principle beyond repetition and relativity, and is intended as a reminder of the ultimate goal of the journey that man embarks upon.

Potent temple sites

Hindu Asia abounds in sacred places, the potent sites where gods dwell or where they might reveal themselves. The locations of these sites are attractively described in many ancient texts: 'the gods always play where groves are, near rivers, mountains and springs and in towns with pleasure-gardens', states the *Brihatsamhita*. Temples are built at such places to gain the full benefit of resident auspicious deities. When the temple is completed and consecrated the potential sacredness of the site manifests itself and the distinction between artificially and naturally sacred places disappears. The principal features associated with these sites are water, shade and seclusion. The importance attached to these features indicates that they also came to be objects of worship.

Rivers are sacred, especially the Ganges which issues from the mountain of Shiva, and are celebrated for their healing and purifying powers, as are innumerable springs and lakes. Waters are identified with their most characteristic flower, the lotus, an ever popular symbol in Hinduism for renewal and enlightenment. Water is also necessary for the successful functioning of the temple as it is required for ritual ablutions. Where no river, spring or lake is available, artificial cisterns or reservoirs are constructed in which water is preserved in times of rain. Tree cults, common the world over among many cultures, are widespread in Hinduism where every village and town has its sacred tree or grove. These shady locations are always considered to be places where meditation is possible and at which contact with the divine may be successfully achieved.

In the sacred geography of Hinduism every natural feature is invested with significance by mythology and folklore. Certain sites are associated with a particular exploit or appearance of a god or goddess, for example the places in northern India where the god Krishna made his earthly appearances and those where the *yoni* and other parts of Parvati fell to earth after she had flung herself into flames. There hardly exists in Hindu Asia a temple that does not have some legend attached to it to explain the holiness of its location. Archaeology demonstrates that the sacredness of the site frequently survived changes of cult through the centuries. Some of these legends may perhaps have been intended to justify the sanctity of sites whose original divine associations had been forgotten or were no longer considered appropriate. Potential sanctity of a site is also related to the calendar, in that only at certain times in the year may it be manifested, thus providing an opportunity for ceremony and festival.

Mountain, cave and cosmic axis

The gods of Hinduism are always attracted to mountains and caves, and these geographical features have great importance for the symbolism and outer appearance of the temple. That the temple itself is considered a mountain is indicated by the names, Meru and Kailasa, that may be given to actual temples (Fig. 80). Demonstrated in a temple so designated is a specific desire to identify it with these celebrated mythological mountains. Thus, the temple becomes an architectural facsimile of the sacred places of the gods, providing for the worshipper the merit that would be his through an actual visit to the mountains. Meru is the centre or 'navel' of the universe, standing as a reference point for the surrounding and concentrically arranged continents, oceans and heavenly bodies. Kailasa is the celestial abode of Shiva, the supreme mountain god. In the superstructure of the Hindu temple, perhaps its most characteristic feature, the identification of the temple with the mountain is specific and the superstructure itself is known as a 'mountain peak' or 'crest' (*shikhara*). The curved contours of some temple superstructures and their tiered arrangements owe much to a desire to suggest the visual effect of a mountain peak (Fig. 62). The development of building techniques—in stone, brick and timber—permitted architects to realize increasingly complex schemes for the superstructures of temples, and there was a particular impulse to extend upwards to create soaring towers. The horizontal tiers or storeys which appear on the superstructures of temples are referred to as 'earth' or 'soil' (*bhumi*) in the architectural terminology of ancient texts on temple building, as if to further reinforce this mountain symbolism. In the reduplicating superstructure systems of some Hindu temples, spectacularly developed in the north Indian style, can be seen a conscious attempt to create in stone a complete mountain range.

The cave is a most enduring image in Hinduism, functioning both as a place of retreat and as the occasional habitation of the gods. Caves must always have been felt to be places of great sanctity and they were sometimes enlarged to provide places of worship. Thus came about the practice of excavating into rock to create man-made grottos which were believed to be as sacred as their natural prototypes (Fig. 44). In fact, architects in India only turned to free-standing stone architecture with the greatest reluctance. Such hesitation is not satisfactorily explained merely in terms of technical inexperience with structural stonework, but reflects the survival of the symbolic power of the image of the cave in matters of sacred architecture. In all Hindu temples the sanctuary is strongly reminiscent of a cave; it is invariably small and dark as no natural light is permitted to enter, and the surfaces of the walls are unadorned and massive. Penetration towards the image or symbol of the deity housed in this setting is always through a progression from light into darkness, from open and large spaces to a confined and small space. This movement from complexity of visual experience to that of simplicity may be interpreted by the devotee as a progression of increasing sanctity culminating in the focal point of the temple, the cave or 'womb'.

Accompanying this penetration inwards towards the cave is the ascent upwards to the symbolic mountain peak, whose summit is positioned over the centre of the cave-sanctuary. This means that the highest point of the elevation of the temple is aligned with the most sacred part of the temple, the centre of the inner sanctuary which houses the image of the god. Summit and sacred centre are linked together along an axis which is a powerful projection upwards of the forces of energy which radiate from the centre of the sanctuary (Fig. 26). The movement upwards is both visual and symbolic, since it dominates the external appearance of the temple and is associated with certain ideas about the universe. The Hindu imagination supplies various associations with this ascent along an axis which is likened to a progression towards enlightenment, and the goal of this journey is identified with the crowning finial of the superstructure of the temple. The mechanical conception of the cosmos identifies the axis with the support of the heavens, the central mountain Meru. The biological viewpoint transforms this axis into an ever-living trunk of a tree supporting the universe in its ample branches. The anthropomorphic approach imagines the cosmic man (*mahapurusha*) displaying the whole of creation on his body, providing a

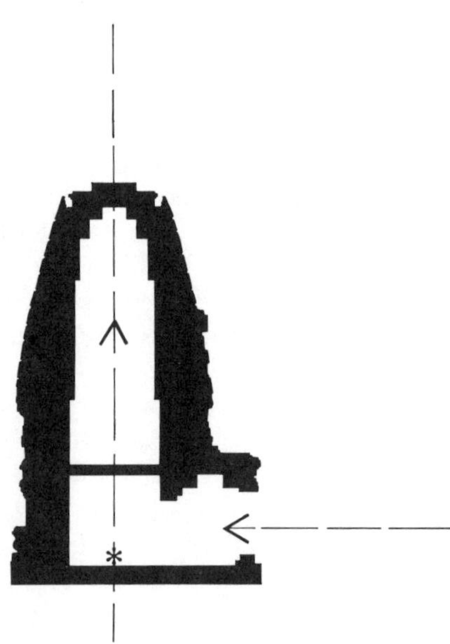

26 Relation of the symbolic images of cave, mountain and cosmic axis in the temple section: the summit of the temple is directly above the sacred centre

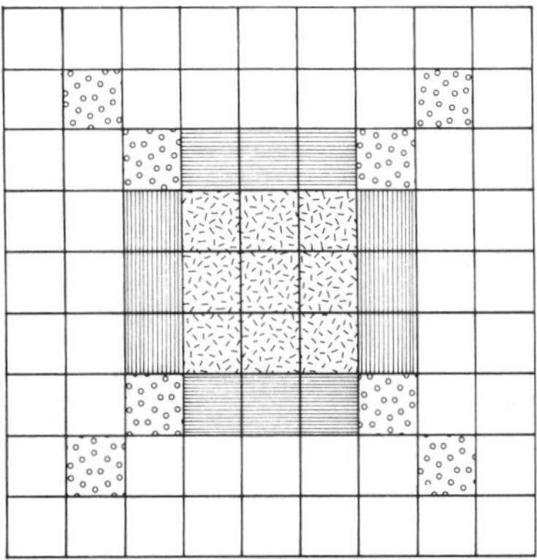

27 The *mandala* governing the temple plan, following the *Brihatsamhita*, a text dating from the Gupta period. Brahma occupies the central nine squares and is surrounded by various planetary divinities, including the Sun and Moon

means of access to the higher and more sacred spheres through his spine which is identified with the vertical axis. Also of significance is the pillar (*yupa*) associated with kingship and royal proclamations; cosmic support is another function of this pillar, which keeps apart the earth and sky. In one of the most celebrated of Hindu myths the world mountain is specifically identified with a churning axis or pillar. Vertical ascent and cosmic axis, therefore, are all bound up with ideas about the composition of the universe.

The cosmology of the temple plan

Once the site of the temple has been selected and ritually purified, the next stage in its erection is the laying out of the ground plan. Great importance is attached to the establishment of the temple's ground plan because it functions as a sacred geometric diagram (*mandala*) of the essential structure of the universe. The mandala is a concentric figuration, usually a square divided into a number of smaller squares by an intersecting grid of lines. This arrangement of central squares with others that surround it is taken to be a microscopic image of the universe with its concentrically organized structure (Fig. 27). By constructing this diagram to regulate the form of the temple, a symbolic connection is created, binding together the world of the gods—the universe, and its miniature reconstruction through the work of man—the temple. The assumption permitting such an identification of the universe with its model is that of a spatial and physical correspondence between the worlds of god and man.

The mandala of the temple plan is also considered a symbolic pantheon of the gods, as the smaller squares of the diagram are each the seat of a particular deity. The central and largest square is usually occupied by Brahma or some other prominent deity concerned with creation. Arranged around this square are the planetary divinities, the guardians of the directions of

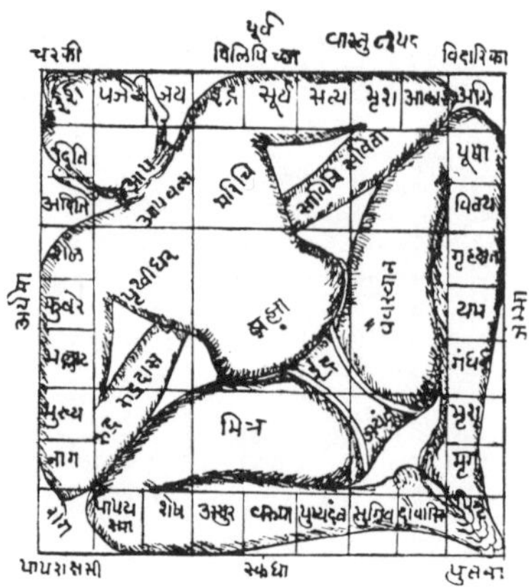

28 The cosmic man, *mahapurusha*, drawn on a temple *mandala*, from an ancient manual of architecture

space, and other astronomical deities. The mandala is thus able to incorporate the courses of the heavenly bodies which are related to all recurring time sequences. It may also contain an image of the cosmic man arranged diagonally, each square connected with some portion of his body. This cosmic figure is identified with the processes of the creation of the universe and its underlying structure (Fig. 28).

Profound significance is attached to the centre of the temple mandala, as it is here that the worshipper may experience transformation as he comes into direct contact with the cosmic order. The centre is the most sacred part of the diagram and is materialized in Hindu temple architecture by the image or symbol of the divinity placed in the sanctuary. In the cosmological interpretation of the plan the centre coincides with the sacred mountain, Meru, the support of the universe. In ritual the dynamics of the temple all proceed with reference to this central point; symbolic processes of interpreting the form of the temple all focus upon the centre of the plan.

Set rules attend the laying out of the temple mandala before the commencement of building operations. In order that the temple should be able to function effectively the moment when the diagram is drawn upon the ground has to be accurately and suitably determined. Here the relation between time and architecture is introduced, in which the observation of the heavenly bodies bears upon temple building. Astronomy and astrology, never truly separated in Hinduism, provide the basis for determining the appropriate moments when all important activities are undertaken. The *Brihatsamhita*, one of the early sources of information about temple building, is actually a treatise on astrology which includes a chapter on architecture. Not only is the moment in time determined at which the plan of the temple is laid out, but the regulating mandala itself is a product of astronomical calculations. Characteristic is the symbolism of the cardinal points of the compass and the orientation of the mandala according to the course of the sun. The plan of the temple is strictly orientated to the cardinal directions, usually along an east-west axis. Of great importance in the architectural texts, the Shastras and Agamas, are the detailed sections giving astrological-astronomical information. Here is expressed a conscious desire to identify the physical forms of the temple with the laws that govern the movements of heavenly bodies.

Sacred mathematics

In Hindu thought number is considered an expression of the structure of the universe and a means of effecting the interplay between the universe and man. Mathematical schemes are frequently constructed by the philosophers and theologians of Hinduism to describe the celestial, terrestrial and even the ethical worlds. In the Hindu temple mathematics has a peculiar significance. A common word used to designate a temple, *vimana*, means that which is 'well-measured' or 'well-proportioned'. Textbooks on temple building all devote lengthy chapters to the subject of proportional measurement, describing in detail different systems which are intended to control every dimension of the temple—the length and width of its plan, the extent of its internal spaces and even the measurements of such details as doorways and base mouldings. The proportional systems have as their outstanding feature the use of a unit of measurement sometimes known as the 'finger' (*angula*), from which are derived the dimensions of the sanctuary or the height of the image of the deity housed there. This then regulates the masses of the temple as they extend upwards and outwards from the sanctuary. Every part of the temple, therefore, is rigorously controlled by a proportional system of measurement and interrelated by the use of the fundamental unit.

Only if the temple is constructed correctly according to a mathematical system can it be expected to function in harmony with the mathematical basis of the universe. The inverse of this belief is also held: an architectural text, the *Mayamata*, adds that 'if the measurement of the temple is in every way perfect, there will be perfection in the universe as well'. Thus the welfare of the community and the happiness of its members depend upon the correctly proportioned temple, and architectural texts stress that only work that is completed 'according to the rules' will gain the desired merit for its builder.

Measurement in the Hindu temple is not confined to the architecture. The sacred images of the temple, whether carved or painted, are also subject to strict mathematical control in the discipline of iconometry, the geometry of image-making. The *Shukranatisara*, an iconographical text, states that an image is 'said to be lovely which is neither more nor less than the prescribed proportions'; another text warns that 'the image not made with the prescribed rules . . . is fruitless and its worship is without any effect'. Only a well executed image, satisfactory in its proportional measurements, will be able to invite the deity to reside within it. Various canons of proportions are discovered in the texts on image-making which mostly propose the face-length as the module (*tala*) for the figure. The systematic ordering of icons

29 *Above* Doorway to the Dashavatara temple, Deogarh, sixth century, showing the river goddesses elevated at either side, guardians, protective couples and auspicious female figures
30 *Right* Ritual sexual exhibitionism—the Kandariya Mahadeva temple, Khajuraho, eleventh century

according to their measurements is accompanied by equally particular classifications based upon facial expression, posture, hand gesture, costume, ornament and colour.

Protection of the temple

The sanctity of the temple naturally requires protection at all times from unwanted negative forces, sometimes personified as evil spirits or demons. In fact, the whole programme of erecting a temple is replete with rituals to provide adequate protection at vulnerable moments in the building process,

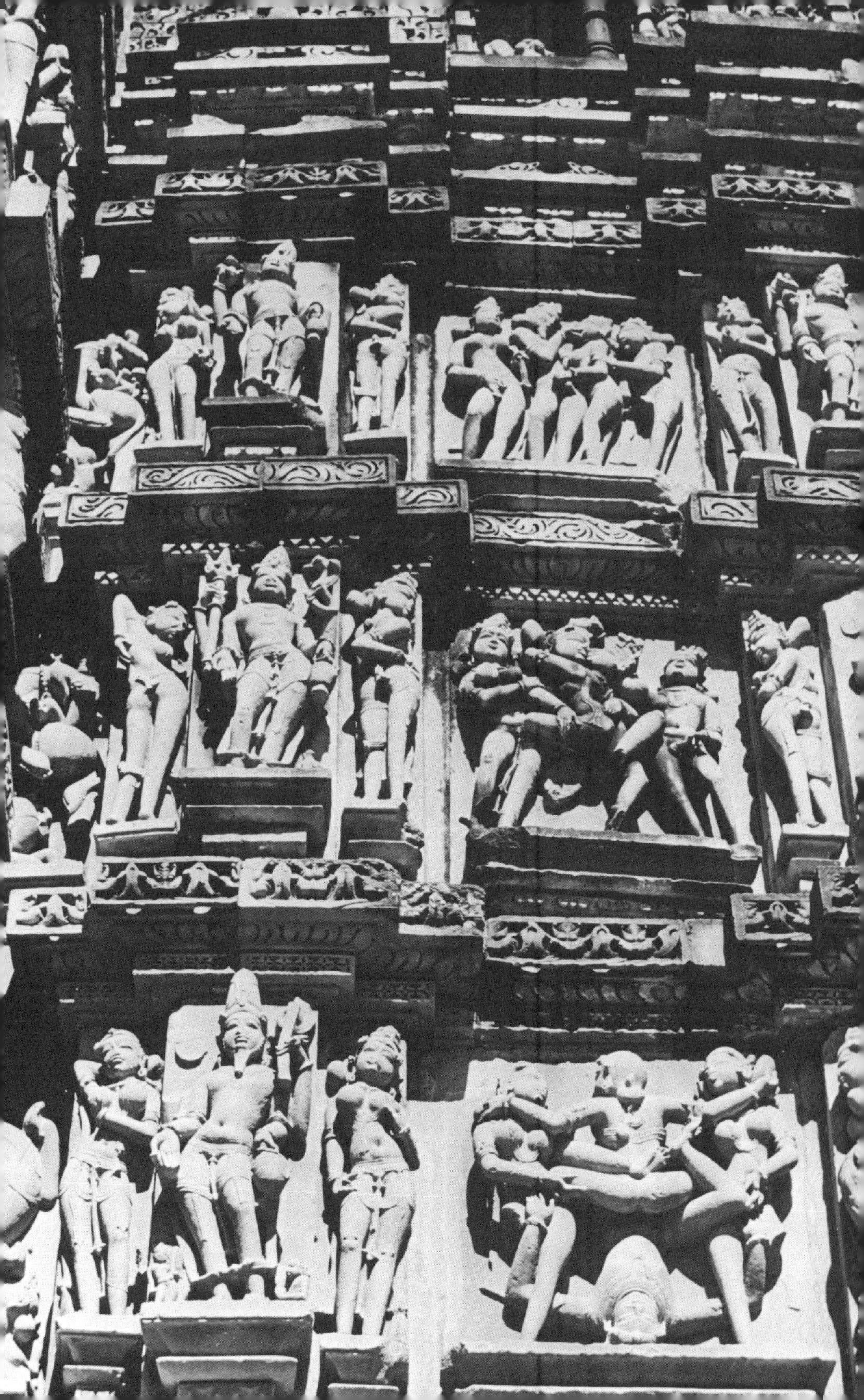

in particular the selection of the site, the drawing of the plan upon the ground, the laying of the foundation stones, and the final stage of building when the finial is placed on the summit of the superstructure. When completed, the temple continues to need protection as a place where the power of the divinity radiates outwards for the benefit of the community. The symbolic processes that permit the temple to be identified with the scheme of the cosmos and with the world of the gods are also in need of beneficial influences.

Many of the rituals performed in the temple are undertaken for the sake of security and as a source of prosperity and good health for the worshipper. Likewise, much of the art in the temple functions in this dual role. This is particularly true of the motifs and images that decorate the doorway or entrance to a temple or enclosure, the most vulnerable part of a sacred structure and the one most in need of protection from evil forces, real or invisible (Fig. 29). Protection is also required at the most critical moment in the fashioning of a sacred image—the carving or painting of the eyes of the image which are then 'opened'. At this point the image becomes a potential receptacle for the divinity. The magical aspect of Hindu temple art is seen in the numerous minor deities, guardians and attendant figures that surround the sacred image once it is installed, their powers of protection emanating from them. Coupled figures and demonic masks also appear as part of the repertoire of motifs which function in a protective manner.

Among the motifs that provide protection in the Hindu temple are erotic female images, the displayed female *yoni*, and ritual sexual exhibitionism in which the conjunction of male and female is stressed (Fig. 30). The only convincing explanation for the constant appearance of these motifs throughout the history of Hindu temple architecture as decoration, especially at doorways, would seem to be that they function as ornamentation imbued with magical powers. The fact that erotic images are continually found on temples, whereas other decorative motifs may be omitted, suggests that eroticism has a uniquely auspicious significance. Almost certainly this significance is bound up with the protection of the temple and the continuance and well-being of the community which it serves. The same is true of many of the other motifs that recur in Hindu temple art. From the Vedas onwards, Indian religion is full of prayers for the propagation of life and survival of the community. This is the cogent explanation for the copulating figures and emblems of fertility found on Hindu temples. Even sexual deviations, where they are depicted in the art of the temple, are an expression of life, which above all the Hindu temple embodies.

PART TWO

The Forms of the Temple

5 The Science of Building

The earliest Indian records of the ancient Hindu science of building (*vastu*) are contemporary with the beginnings of temple building from the fourth century onwards and form chapters in the larger Epics and Puranas. In later centuries compendia of architectural information form complete works, the *Vastushastras*, in which many aspects of building, sculpture and painting are gathered together. From the language in which these works are written and the fragmentary nature of much of the information they contain, it appears that the known Shastras are more likely to be the theoretical writings of theologians, the learned brahmans, than manuals of architectural and artistic practice compiled by builders and craftsmen. Those directly involved with the creation of the temples, their sculptures and their paintings, usually had no need to set down their traditions in writing as the knowledge of building techniques was imparted from one generation to the next. The function of recording architectural and artistic practice was largely left to the brahmans, who attempted to control the processes of design and execution by setting them down in writing. The Shastras are mostly compilations of several different architectural and artistic traditions and aspire to an encyclopedic survey of all that is known. However, they are frequently obscure in their terminology and fragmentary in the information they impart; it would seem that their compilers were always one stage removed from building practice. In fact, the Shastras are rarely concerned with the process of erecting temples and most of their information about building practice relies upon the evidence of the temples themselves. The lack of technical information in the Shastras reveals their true function as a collection of rules which attempt to facilitate the translation of theological concepts into architectural forms. The early texts, furthermore, indicate a concern with all aspects of secular building as well as sacred, and contain material on fortifications, the layout of cities, and military equipment.

Materials

'Stone or wood is worthy of the gods, brahmans, kings and hermits, but unsuited to *vaishyas* and *shudras*', recommends the *Mayamata*, an early text on temple building. In this way the materials of the temple are directly related to the classes of Hindu society. Other Shastras, however, permit the use of stone as a material for all temples, irrespective of who builds them or worships there. On occasion, the colours of the building materials are related to the different strata of Hindu society—white stone is to be used by brahmans, red by *kshatriyas*, yellow by *vaishyas* and black by *shudras*. These colours may also apply to other materials. Some Shastras identify the materials of the temple with gender: thus, stone and brick are considered suitable for a temple dedicated to a male deity, while a building in brick and wood is appropriate for a female divinity. If all three materials are combined then the temple is neuter. Many texts strongly recommend stone as the most sacred of building materials—'it is a hundred times more meritorious to build a temple in brick than to build one in wood . . . it is even ten thousand times more meritorious to build a temple in stone than in brick.' As soon as the building materials are removed from their natural environment they are freed from all former associations by the performance of certain rites. The felling of trees, baking of bricks or quarrying of stone initiates the process by which the materials of the temple eventually come to be identified with the body of the god or goddess who temporarily resides in it. The Shastras prohibit the re-use of materials from ruined temples as these have already been given identity and could function effectively only in their original context; they insist on the use of materials made or collected expressly for a new building, otherwise impurities might enter the building. However, older materials were in fact frequently re-used in temple building.

Temples continued to be built during all periods in Hindu Asia from timber, mud and plaster, though large and important buildings usually employed the more durable brick or stone. Brick building was the earliest technique to gain popularity, and remains of brick structures in India date back to the centuries before the Christian era in Buddhist, Jain and Hindu architecture. Brick and mortar continued to be preferred for Hindu temples in those areas of India which were dominated by brick traditions and which had a scarcity of suitable available stone. Central and eastern India, the Himalayas as well as parts of mainland South-East Asia and the Indonesian archipelago preserve brick building traditions to the present day.

It is in stone that Hindu architecture develops its most characteristic expression. The technique employed is either that of excavating into solid rock, or drystone structural masonry in which stone blocks are laid one upon another without any use of mortar. The highly evolved techniques of excavating and cutting blocks of stone constitute one of the major technical achievements associated with the history of the Hindu temple, both in India and in other parts of Hindu Asia. Variations in the quality of the stone available account for differences in the carving techniques and decorative forms evolved: thus, the hard and brilliant granite employed by the Pallava builders in the seventh and eighth centuries, the finely grained yellow sandstone of central India used by the architects of the temples erected under the Chandellas in the tenth and eleventh centuries, and the soft and volcanic stone common in Java and Bali all had their impact upon the sharpness of architectural detail and the modelling of carved decoration and sacred images. Most stone buildings were probably covered with a thin layer of plaster which was usually coloured, but no temple of any antiquity has survived with its original coloured surface. This layer of plaster was useful for unifying parts of the building executed in different materials. Countless

31 Ladkhan temple, Aihole, seventh century. The sloping roofs reproduce in stone the forms of thatch and timber

examples of temple architecture in southern India simultaneously utilized granite and brick, whose different textures were concealed by this plaster coating.

Timber origins of Indian architecture

The ground plans of Indian brick buildings from as early as the second century BC often involve curvatures which were achieved with facility in brick, and later in rock-hewn architecture. Wood and flexible timber or bamboo traditions are also characterized by the versatility of their building forms, and examples of these structures are found in a number of representations in the relief carvings and paintings of early Indian art. The very impermanence of timber architecture probably promoted a degree of innovation which resulted in a variety of architectural forms. In fact, many of the traditional Hindu temple models are directly derived from wood and bamboo architecture, and this is especially evident in many roof forms and window shapes that have curved contours; among these are the popular horseshoe arched window placed in the roof, the apse, and the ribbed barrel vault.

Indian architectural history in stone opens with a series of Buddhist sanctuaries entirely excavated into rock—usually an escarpment or cliff—whose cavernous interiors have ceilings of a raftered character. In the relatively early examples at various sites in western India dating from the first century BC, heavy cross-beams and raftered frameworks are found, either as actual timber beams or as rock-cut copies. This clearly demonstrates that the original architectural models, of which these artificial caves are facsimiles, were built in light and pliable materials, either flat-roofed or vaulted. Wooden details also influenced the elements of stone and brick architecture such as doorway and column design and roof forms (Fig. 31). The rich carvings of lintels and jambs of doorway openings quite clearly indicate the original timber joinery, with the projecting lintel copied in stone.

Cutting and carving in stone

Indian rock-cut sanctuaries date from as early as the third and second centuries BC, and the technique of cutting into rock to create artificial cave-temples was to influence Indian architectural practice for over a thousand years. Most of the early rock-cut sanctuaries were utilized by Buddhist and Jain sects and their changing forms follow the development of these religions through a variety of phases. Their interior spaces are skilfully and often elaborately organized and the range of sculptural images and motifs with which they are decorated, together with their painted surfaces, indicates the emergence of craftsmen who were later to be concerned with the decoration of the Hindu temple.

The methods employed of carving directly into stone are revealed in those caves that were never completed. The nature of the tools that were used can only be inferred from the traces they left behind in the rock; they would appear chiefly to have been a pointed chisel and an iron mallet. First of all the rock face was polished with iron chisels and the façade of the sanctuary sketched in and incised. If a high chamber was to be hewn out of the rock the workmen commenced by driving a tunnel as tall as a man into the rock beneath the place where the ceiling would be. This was then widened and deepened by cutting steps. On each level the stonemason who did the rough work was followed by another artisan who cleaned and polished the walls. Some of the incomplete caves at Mahabalipuram, begun under Pallava patronage in the seventh century, provide information about the technique used to hollow out low chambers. The artisans incised the colonnade on the polished rock of the façade and divided up the remaining area which had to be worked into a square panel. Deep grooves were then cut along the incised lines with a pointed chisel so as to leave regular protuberances which were then easily hewn off. When the first layer was removed the process was repeated until the chamber reached the required depth. Only when the entire rock-cut

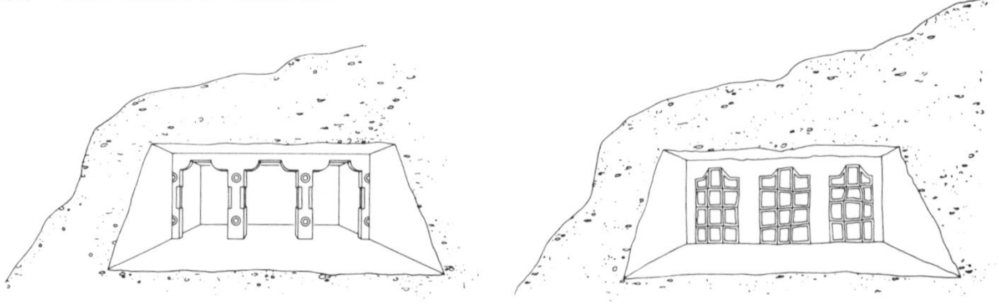

32 Creating a rock-cut temple, Mahabalipuram, seventh century. The colonnade is incised and grooves are cut to leave protuberances which are then hewn off

temple had been given a roughly hewn shape did artisans set to work to polish the walls and columns (Fig. 32).

In the early development of the structural Hindu temple there were a great many features which were borrowed from rock-cut architecture. At some sites in India both structural and rock-cut techniques were employed at the same time. Towards the end of their rock-cut phase in the seventh century, Pallava architects initiated the practice of carving rock to produce monolithic facsimiles of structural temples; the '*rathas*' at Mahabalipuram are among the most celebrated Indian examples (Fig. 33). The favoured technique of carving a building was still adhered to even after temples were erected in structural stonework. The mass of the temple and sanctuary was usually built from rectangular-shaped stone slabs from which was created an approximate and quasi-monolithic temple form. Stonemasons then chiselled this to achieve the carved outline of the features of the temple. Because of this method the joints between the stones only occasionally and haphazardly coincided with architectonic forms, running slantwise over cornices or cutting through pilasters. The same was true for images and ornamental motifs which were frequently carved across the joints (Fig. 7). The fact that stones were finely carved so as to achieve an almost invisible jointing system only enhanced the massive quasi-monolithic quality of the structural stone temple.

Another leading feature found throughout the history of Hindu temple architecture is the emphasis on the carving of surface ornamentation as the principal visual language. Carving lies at the very root of the endeavour of the Hindu artist, and architecture itself is considered as a mass which requires sculpturing. In fact, carving the surface of the building is always preferred to structural innovation which is usually deliberately rejected. In this respect Hindu architecture is directly opposed to Gothic architecture.

Brick and stone construction

The fundamental architectural principle of the constructed Hindu temple is always formulated in the trabeate order by which only horizontal and vertical members are employed, stability being given by massive arrangements of vertical elements such as pillars and pilasters together with equally heavy cross-beams and lintels. The most characteristic features of this post and beam method of construction are the techniques employed to span openings and enclose interior spaces. Most openings in Hindu temples are bridged with a single member, a lintel either of stone or timber, and interior spaces are covered by slabs of stone, usually laid horizontally (though sometimes inclined roof-slabs are preferred) spanning from one supporting beam or wall to another (Fig. 49). The post and beam construction method is extended by a development of corbelling techniques, by which stones or bricks in each horizontal course are progressively projected out to cause the gap between two walls to diminish until it can be closed with a single stone or brick.

Factors of functional engineering principle never really played a part in the evolution of Hindu temple architecture. The pillar-lintel-corbel scheme of construction is at the root of all Hindu temple building operations and other structural principles such as the cantilever and the dome are only of the most rudimentary nature. Thus, the fixture of the eave which projects from the wall, and which involves the cantilever principle, never develops any true structural application in the Hindu architectural context. Arrangements of internal ceilings are also deliberately confined to the overlapping of one stone course with another or, alternatively, to the laying of diagonal and square stone courses to produce designs with rotating and diminishing squares (Fig. 34). Sometimes circular stone courses are employed, seated one above the other in receding diameters, to produce complex designs—well

33 Dharmaraja '*ratha*', Mahabalipuram, seventh century: the lower portions are incomplete

34 Ceiling of Shiva temple, Pandrethan, ninth or tenth century: this design is related to ceilings of other temples that have cosmological symbolism

exploited, for example, in the tenth- and eleventh-century temples of Rajasthan and Gujarat. Never was the principle of the arch with radiating components, such as voussoirs and keystones, employed in Hindu structures, either in India or in other parts of Asia. It was not so much that Hindu architects were ignorant of these techniques, but rather that conformance to tradition and adherence to precedents were firm cultural attitudes. Arched niches, where found, are created on the surface of a wall or tower and rarely carry loads from above as in the true arch. This also means that Hindu temple architecture provides no instance of the use of the vault or the dome. It is only the corbelled structural device that is used, always in its non-arched form, to create the interiors of temples and the stone shells of the superstructures that rise above the sanctuary. The preference of Hindu architects is for massiveness and strength in temple construction through the post and beam method.

In the erection of the structural temple an organized building programme was followed. Bricks were baked either on or near the site and stone was mostly quarried locally. From reliefs carved on temples and from a manuscript that has been discovered about the building operations carried out at the thirteenth-century Surya temple at Konarak it is learnt that stone from quarries was sometimes transported to the building site on wooden rollers drawn by elephants or floated on barges along rivers and canals. At the site the masons roughly shaped the stone blocks which were then hoisted into position by rope pulleys on scaffolding; ramps were also constructed of timber or sand to facilitate the placing of extremely heavy members in place. The division of work into different phases corresponded to the tasks of different craftsmen such as stonemasons, carvers and sculptors. To secure stone slabs firmly together, iron clamps and wedges were utilized. This permitted the occasional virtuoso development of corbelling in which horizontal stone layers were projected out over large spans and cut into unusual shapes to produce highly decorative ceiling schemes. Occasionally, as in the Surya temple at Konarak, iron beams were used in the sanctuary and hall. Stone columns were at all times important supporting members, and most structural systems were built up with columns supporting principal beams upon which rested secondary beams running at right angles to them. These secondary beams, usually shorter than those beneath, were sometimes repeated in order to create continuous rising structural systems. Timber was always used for doors, and for windows timber bars were skilfully copied in pierced stone screens.

6 Temple Styles

Differences in language and culture have always existed between the river plains of northern India and the peninsula to the south, and the earliest surviving brick and stone temples going back to the fifth and sixth centuries are clearly divided into the broad categories of 'northern' and 'southern' styles. The most easily recognizable difference between temples built in these two styles are seen in the shapes of their superstructures. But there are further variants which extend into all aspects of temple architecture—the plan, vertical profile, repertoire of ornamental motifs, and even the programme of sacred images considered suitable for the outer walls and interior spaces of the temple—which make for two completely demarcated temple styles.

All of northern India, from the foothills of the Himalayas to the central plateau of the Deccan, from Gujarat in the west to Orissa and Bengal in the east, is furnished with temples in the northern style. The great expanse of this area accounts for the clearly differentiated regional variations within the style. In contrast the southern style, confined to the most southerly portions of the subcontinent, was much more consistent in its development. At certain periods there occurred striking juxtapositions of the two architectural styles as influences from different regions confronted each other. This is particularly found in the temples of the Early Chalukyas whose kingdom was strategically positioned in the middle of the peninsula in the seventh and eighth centuries. Furthermore, the two styles were not always exclusive; hybrid styles were evolved in the Deccan and the Andhra country. In fact, the history of Hindu temple forms involves considerable stylistic confusion and overlapping, the distribution of the two styles of architecture being moulded as much by historical events as by geography.

Representations of early timber architecture depicted on the stone reliefs of early Buddhist monuments indicate that the coalescence of architectural features into distinct 'northern' and 'southern' styles had not occurred in the centuries immediately preceding the Christian era. The examples that might reveal the original polarization of architectural features into separate styles have yet to be discovered, and the earliest brick and stone temples that have been preserved in India clearly display features of the two broad styles. The range of stylistic variations that emerged as the Hindu temple evolved in different parts of India shows a wealth of inventiveness in the creation of sacred architectural schemes and their decoration, but the unifying characteristics that are inherent in these stylistic developments attest to the essentially conventional and conservative character of Indian architectural and artistic traditions.

35 Stone models of temples illustrating the two styles identified with the terms *nagara* or *prasada* (northern style) and *dravida* or *vimana* (southern style), seventh or eighth century

The stylistic development of the Hindu temple is often traced with the aid of such terms as 'classical' and 'medieval', by which a sense of chronology and architectural evolution is communicated. Early Hindu temples are characterized by an imaginative variation in the treatment of basic architectural formulae as well as decorative themes, and up to the seventh and eighth centuries a certain simplicity of form is coupled with considerable virtuosity in technique, especially in stone carving. The term 'classical' is often applied to this formative period, which is distinguished from the following phase of temple evolution, extending up to the twelfth and thirteenth centuries and beyond, sometimes referred to as 'medieval'. The stylistic characteristics that emerged during this latter period are bound up with large-scale building projects in which the ritual consolidations of Hindu cults resulted in clear artistic standardizations. The stylistic diagnostic of 'classical' as opposed to 'medieval' is mainly identified with inherent stylistic processes such as growth, maturity and decay, and frequently implies judgements of a qualitative nature. Such associations are inappropriate for the architecture of Hinduism because they do not take into account the innate conservative character of Indian artistic traditions, in which stylistic evolution can only be formulated within given architectural models which are basically unaltered over many centuries. These terms, therefore, are not utilized here, for purposes of either description or aesthetic criticism.

Classification of temples

The most outstanding feature of the ancient texts on Hindu architecture, the Shastras, is their classification of the temples into different 'orders'. The terms *nagara*, *dravida* and *vesara* which are found in these texts do not function as all-embracing stylistic categories, but indicate a general impulse to classify temples according to their typological features. Actually, these terms describe temples that primarily employ square, octagonal or apsidal-ended shapes for their plans, these shapes regulating other parts of the temple including its vertical profile. These three shapes are sometimes joined by two more—the ellipse and the rectangle—to produce the five listed in the *Brihatsamhita*. *Nagara* and *dravida* temples are mostly identified with the northern and southern temple styles respectively, as are the further categories of *prasada* and *vimana* temples which also appear in most textual classifications (Fig. 35). Each temple style has its own distinct technical language, though some terms are common but applied to different parts of the building in each style. Thus *shikhara* refers to the whole superstructure in the northern style, but only to the finial of the superstructure in the southern style. This stylistic terminology is accompanied by distinct systems of proportionate measurement. In the description of southern temples the Shastras take into account such variants as buildings whose elevations are based upon a single unit or a number of units vertically superimposed; temples with unlimited and progressive series of units are also described. For northern temples, the Shastras list the horizontal divisions of the vertical profile of the building, from the base to the superstructure and its finial, and classify temples according to these divisions, elaborated in the later texts into many sub-parts.

Regional traditions

The mutual impact of styles of craftsmanship belonging to different Hindu kingdoms was of the greatest importance in the history of Hindu sacred architecture, with regard to the continuing process of innovation and stylistic development. Among the principal factors underlying the styles of craftsmanship were the availability of raw materials and the influence of climate. Raw materials naturally played a dominant role in the techniques of construction and carving. The sources of raw materials were not always found within the confines of a kingdom, although sometimes more than one material was available locally. Contrasting artistic traditions were developed in areas where the quality of stone varied: thus, hard and crystalline rocks prevented detailed carving, whereas soft and sedimentary stone permitted great precision. Friable and schist-like stones, such as those employed by the Hoyshala architects in the twelfth and thirteenth centuries (Fig. 83), promoted the carving of mouldings created by sharp and angled incisions. Brick building traditions continued to survive where there was an absence of good stone, and techniques of moulding and carving bricks doubtless influenced the style of temples in these areas (Fig. 90). Each building material, together with its tonal value, texture and structural possibilities, was therefore to affect local traditions.

The influence of climate, too, is clear. In the relatively heavy rainfall areas of the western coast of India temples have sloping tiled roofs, giving rise to timber gables. To overcome the hazards of snow and hail, wooden sloped roofs are also employed in the temples of the Himalayan valleys (Fig. 68), and similar forms are found in the sloping thatched roofs of Java and Bali which lie well within the tropical zone (Fig. 97). In general, the hotter and drier the climate, the flatter the roof; open porches provide shaded seating, and pierced stone screens are utilized to filter the light.

Building a temple was frequently the product of the religious fervour of the monarch who ruled the region, and generally it did not matter to which cult of Hinduism his beliefs were affiliated as differences in Hindu temple styles never coincided with variations of cult. The direct association of royalty with the building of temples was a persistent historical phenomenon in Hindu Asia and had a pronounced effect upon the stylistic development of the temple, the zeal of the royal patron fostering the rise of regional style by the encouragement given to local craftsmen. Indeed, many of the regional styles of Hindu temples may be identified by dynastic appellations: the temples resolve themselves into such groups as Gupta, Chalukya, Kalinga, Chandella, Pallava, Chola and Hoyshala. The same is also true for temples outside India. Royal conquests and other forms of political contacts were important media for the dispersal of regional cultural impulses. Political rivalry among the Hindu kingdoms of India and South-East Asia stimulated the possibility of interflow between artistic centres, and kings vied with each other in erecting structures which would outshine edifices in rival kingdoms. There are also numerous recorded instances of artisans being brought from one region to another by victorious kings.

Another significant factor in regional traditions is that of upsurges of religious revivalism, bringing entire communities together in corporate efforts to raise temples. These movements were often linked with political events and were led by dynastic rulers. In western India after the eleventh century, for example, the onslaughts of Islamic invasions brought patrons and craftsmen together in fresh efforts to build temples, as if the sole inspiration was the desire to preserve intact the Hindu religion.

Principles of stylistic evolution

Certain general principles of architectural growth lie behind the categories of 'northern' and 'southern' as well as their original variants. Perhaps the

36 *Above* Roof of the Vishnu temple, Gop, sixth or seventh century, showing the false horseshoe-shaped windows
37 *Right* Detail of the superstructure of the Galaganatha temple, Pattadakal, eighth century. Faces peer out of arched 'windows' which ascend in diminishing storeys

most fundamental stylistic characteristic of Hindu temple architecture is the innate conservatism which governed the choice of architectural forms and decorative motifs. The timber origins of many of the details of temple architecture have already been noted, and it is significant that once these details had become part of a stone tradition they were never to be completely abandoned. This conservatism also explains the retention of old and sometimes obsolete forms and the continued use of forms when the original context was lost. The most spectacular instance of stylistic conservatism is to be seen in the various roof shapes that were reduced to two-dimensional outlines, providing a wealth of shapes by which pediments, lintels or cornices were created. But conservatism did not necessarily imply an absence of innovation, and Indian temples provide ample evidence of an inspired improvisation within well defined architectural formulae. Familiar patterns were continually re-worked—either plan types, superstructure profiles, or particular motifs such as the horseshoe arched window. The latter, for example, was exploited throughout the history of the north Indian temple until its original context as a doorway or dormer window, as may be found in the seventh-century temple at Gop, was forgotten (Fig. 36). This motif was also employed as a frame for a carved image or a surmounting pediment to an opening or niche; it was fragmented into derivative components which were recombined so as to create new patterns in which the original arch was

undetectable; it was also provided with miniature faces which peered outwards so as to preserve its original usage as a window (Fig. 37). Thus, a design originally intended for a doorway or wall niche also functioned as a projection on the superstructure or was superimposed on the mouldings of a plinth. Certain specific mouldings that were once confined to a particular position on the wall, such as the animal friezes that coincided with the ends of the floor-slabs of south Indian temples, came to be moved up the wall. The angled eave characteristic of the north Indian temple, which once belonged only to open porches, was applied to solid walls in order to create divisions or to shelter niches that were treated as if they were miniature ornamental porches. Motifs, too, changed in their usage; the pot and foliage design, at first employed as a capital above a column shaft, was later applied to the bases of columns. In the northern temple style the superstructure profile was shifted down the wall to provide a frame for niches. In the southern style the characteristic parapet was re-used again and again, until its original function—that of continuing the wall above the roof line—no longer dictated its position on the temple elevation.

Repetition is inevitably one of the factors that explain the stylistic evolution of Hindu temples. The rhythmic projections of the temple plan carried into the vertical elevation were created by multiplications of the original central wall projection with which early temples were provided. The southern style temples created their rhythmic wall systems by the repetition of projections that framed recesses, pairs of pilasters marking each change in the wall plane. The northern temple style developed a complex system of breaking up the plane of the wall until the temple plan almost approached a circle. In the vertical elevation of the temple, multiplication of the principal shaft of the superstructure created the complex towered systems in which the central shaft was surrounded by clustered miniature reproductions of itself. The most spectacular examples of these superstructures are seen in the eleventh- and twelfth-century Chandella temples (Fig. 62). In the southern style, temple superstructures repeated the architectonic elements of the main wall beneath, the temple masses rising upwards in a number of storeys (Fig. 81). Essential to both temple styles was the principle by which forms were repeated on different scales so that shapes which were large and indicative of structural context became small and ornamental; these diminutive forms were sometimes combined with the originals from which they were derived. Such stylistic diminutions were at the root of the complex and subtle rhythmic proportional schemes by which the elevations of Hindu temples were organized. Not only did these geometric processes govern the vertical rise of the temple; they were also necessary to its horizontal spread.

Another factor in the stylistic evolution of the Hindu temple was the tendency towards enlarging the scale of sacred buildings, accompanied by an increase in the complexity of architectonic forms and decoration. Monumentalism and gigantism appealed to the architects of temples as well as to their patrons, and it is not difficult to discover connections between magnitude of physical proportion and the temporal ambitions of the founders of temples. Complexity of architectonic forms—especially in plans, external elevations and interior spaces—was also increasingly pursued by architects throughout the history of the Hindu temple, but the increasingly dominant role of surface decoration was sometimes achieved only at the expense of overall architectural form.

In Hindu sacred sculpture a paramount principle has been isolated: 'expanding form'. The process of growth by which forms expand outwards is of the greatest significance for the masses of the temple whose monolithic qualities were never completely abandoned. The rise of the temple profile to create the superstructure was indeed loaded with symbolic connotations, but it also had a very real visual impact. This impact was created by calculated manipulation of the supporting walls and transitional mouldings in order to achieve the desired sweep upwards, which explains the care taken to achieve continuity between the horizontal divisions of plinth, wall surface, cornice, and surmounting superstructure in northern styled temples. In the southern templé the upper layers underwent a skilful diminution so as to create the concave contour which characterized monumental temple gateways from the twelfth century onwards (Fig. 87). It was this visual expansion of forms that dictated so much of the stylistic development of Hindu temple architecture, and the measure of subtlety attained in both architectural styles was the balance achieved between movement and repose, between dynamic and static forms.

7 The Temples of India

Any account of the Hindu temples of India must inevitably proceed according to the basic categories of northern and southern styles under the patronage of various dynasties of rulers. Such a division, however, does not cover the temples of the peripheral areas of the Himalayan valleys, Bengal, and Kerala, or the significant sub-styles of the Deccan, which are also part of the history of Hindu sacred architecture. There is also the problem that no survey, however detailed, can claim to be definitive, as the temples in India of historical and artistic merit have yet to be fully listed, and ancient monuments are still being discovered each year. The following account indicates only the range of building types and stylistic developments that occurred in the subcontinent over some fifteen centuries, and is in no sense comprehensive. Space has been devoted to the formative stages of architectural and artistic evolution in order to explain the later patterns of temple building in India, some of which survive to the present day.

The northern style under the Guptas and their successors (fifth to seventh centuries)

The history of the north Indian temple style opens with the fragments that survive from the architecture of the Gupta rulers who controlled central northern India during the fourth, fifth and sixth centuries. Cultural life under the Guptas was marked by an unprecedented intellectual ferment and creative vitality in all spheres of life and thought. After their decline the balance of political unity in northern India was lost, the area being ruled by a succession of minor dynasties of largely independent political career until the king Harsha succeeded in partially restoring the empire in the early seventh century. It is to this 'post-Gupta' period that the finest examples of early north Indian temple architecture belong.

Of the free-standing stone temples erected during the period of Gupta rule, only those of Sanchi and Tigawa have been completely preserved. These temples define clearly the essential architectural scheme of the north Indian temple. A square sanctuary adjoins a small pillared porch, both of which are elevated on a plinth. The roof of the sanctuary is created by horizontal stone slabs, and there is no tower. The plain wall surfaces are capped by a horizontal moulding which functions as a cornice. The jambs that flank the doorway are divided into vertical bands that continue over the lintel. The columns of the porch have their shafts divided into square, octagonal and sixteen-sided sections with fluted bell or pot and foliage capitals supporting brackets carved with pairs of seated animals.

The only monuments that may definitely be associated with the Gupta

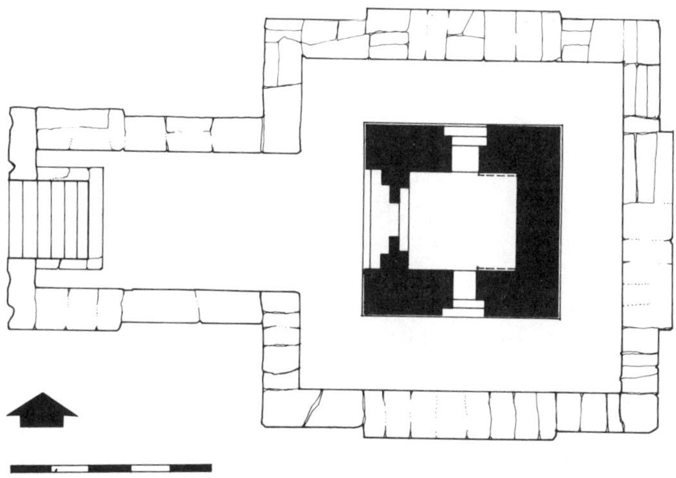

38 Plan of Parvati temple, Nachna, sixth century: the sanctuary is combined with an ambulatory passageway

rulers are the temples and sculptures carved into the sandstone hills at Udaigiri. Of more than twenty excavations forming the group at this site, half consist of rectangular rock-cut shrine chambers. One of these has a structural portico in front of the shrine presenting a façade of columns with a greater span between the innermost pair. Like the columns of the Sanchi and Tigawa temples those at Udaigiri have square, octagonal and sixteen-sided shafts and carry pot and foliage capitals. An identical scheme is employed for the shallow pilasters that frame the doorways of the sanctuaries. This stylistic consistency indicates the emergence of a distinct northern 'order'. The T-shaped doorways have their pilasters set within carved bands that rise up the jambs and over the lintel, decorated with miniature panels of amorous couples and foliage motifs. Images of river goddesses are raised at either side and guardians flank the opening. Elaborate doorway schemes, of which these are the earliest examples, remain a constant feature throughout the history of the north Indian temple.

The precise period to which the temples at Nachna, Bhumara and Deogarh belong is not known for certain, though the stage of their stylistic evolution suggests the sixth century. Unfortunately these buildings are now ruined, the Parvati temple at Nachna and the Dashavatara temple at Deogarh being the best preserved. The plans of these buildings comprise a square sanctuary elevated on a moulded plinth with access by a flight of steps to the east. The Nachna temple is provided with an ambulatory passageway on all four sides of the sanctuary enclosed by walls with pierced stone windows (Fig. 38). At Deogarh there are traces of beams that supported roof-slabs around the sanctuary, but whether these covered a passageway is unclear. Evidence of the development of the northern style is clearly seen in the decoration of the doorways to the sanctuaries of these temples. Probably the most elaborate scheme is the Deogarh doorway, where the characteristic northern style is expressed in its most precise form (Fig. 29). Here the reduced pot and foliage capitals of the pilasters support a lintel which is created from an overhanging eave furnished with horseshoe arched 'windows' which are split into two halves and are surmounted by a complete arch to create a triangular composition—one of the earliest instances of a device that becomes a key feature of the northern style. Over the centre of the doorway is an icon of Vishnu seated on the serpent, indicating the dedication of the sanctuary. The Deogarh temple has the outer sanctuary walls provided with projecting niches which house deeply sculptured panels depicting scenes from the mythology of Vishnu (Fig. 5). The decoration of these niches repeats many of the features of the doorway, including the pilasters which support lotus ornament and a frieze of lion masks.

Doubtless, the fifth and sixth centuries witnessed the emergence of a superstructure rising from the walls of the sanctuary as a distinct characteristic of the northern style. However, in none of these temples are the towers preserved. The Nachna temple has an upper storey with a doorway that appears to be a repetition of the shrine beneath, but its original outer profile has now been lost. At Deogarh, only fragments of the lower portions of the superstructure survive: these indicate a tower similar to those that have been preserved in a complete form in the northern style temples of the Early Chalukyas (Fig. 47).

The temple at Bhitargaon, probably belonging to the fifth century, is a unique example of a brick building from this period with one of the earliest complete superstructures to be preserved in Hindu architecture (Fig. 39). Though there is no true stylistic successor to the Bhitargaon temple it provides important information about early temple forms in the northern style. The temple consists of a square sanctuary with pronounced projections on each side, that to the front extended so as to create a small vestibule for the entrance doorway. The vaulted structure with which the interior spaces are roofed is unparalleled in the history of Hindu building techniques. A high plinth supports the wall which is divided into bays by pilasters whose octagonal shafts have pot-like bases and cushion capitals. The curved brackets support an overhanging curved eave and a terracotta frieze of mythical animals and birds. Between the pilasters of the walls are deep rectangular recesses with moulded terracotta plaques depicting sacred images which reflect a variety of cult affiliations. Above rises the superstructure, with projections that continue those of the walls beneath. Its vertical profile is divided into a number of horizontal layers, each of which has horseshoe-headed niches containing miniature figures or faces.

Two ruined temples from the western and eastern zones of central India attest to the variety of northern Indian architectural forms developed under the successors to the Guptas in the sixth and seventh centuries. The Vishnu temple at Gop in Gujarat is elevated on a plinth divided into bays by a number of pilasters and provided with carved sculptural panels. The temple

39 Brick temple at Bhitargaon, fifth century

itself consists of a square sanctuary with an ambulatory passageway on all four sides whose walls and roofing have now disappeared. The superstructure rises above the sanctuary and has an inclined roof divided into two tiers and capped by a ribbed moulding with an inverted bell profile. Its chief characteristic is the triangular arrangement of false arched windows, two on the lower level with one above, their partly circular forms having foliated

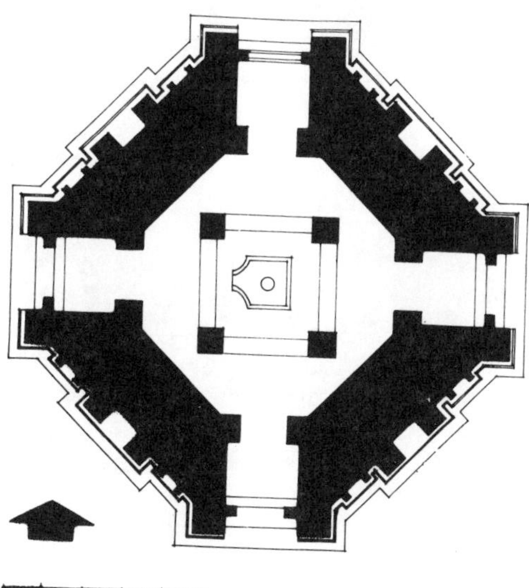

40 Mundeshvari temple, Ramgarh, seventh century: an unusual example of an octagonal plan

'heads' (Fig. 36). They provide one of the only occurrences in stone architecture of full-sized dormer windows projecting from an inclined roof—a feature that is repeated in countless miniature and ornamental variations throughout the history of the northern temple style.

Another unusual seventh-century building is the Mundeshvari temple at Ramgarh in Bihar, whose plan is octagonal in shape, the central interior space combining the requirements of sanctuary and passageway (Fig. 40). Three entrances and a window on the four principal sides of the temple were originally sheltered by porches. The connecting walls have large central niches flanked by smaller niches, provided with their own elaborate plinth mouldings. The entrance doorways and window frames are of the characteristic northern type, as are the pilasters of the niches. Of importance in this temple are the well-preserved smaller niches of the outer walls, which have triangular pediments in which two small arched motifs are surmounted by a larger one distinguished by its trefoil interior.

Rock-cut temples under the Early Chalukyas, Kalachuris and Rashtrakutas (sixth to eighth centuries)

The next phase in the development of the northern temple style is traced in a series of excavated monuments. In the cliffs above Badami, once the capital of the Early Chalukya rulers who dominated much of the Deccan in

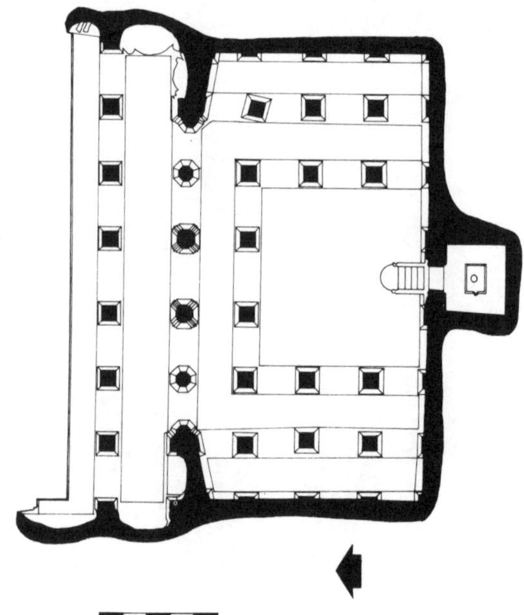

41 *Above* Plan of the Vishnu cave-temple, Badami, sixth century: the sanctuary is positioned in the rear wall of the columned hall

42 *Right* Columns in the Shiva cave-temple, Badami, sixth century

the seventh and early eighth centuries, three excavations were made at the end of the sixth century. These cave-temples are in the form of pillared halls with small cells cut into the rear walls (Figs 41, 42). The halls are noted for their columnar forms which present a variety of types including those with fluted shafts or panels of relief carvings; cushion capitals are also employed. Together with the doorways, these columns display clear northern stylistic characteristics. The brackets of the outer columns of these caves are fashioned to depict amorous couples beneath trees, a motif considered particularly appropriate for the entrance of the temple. The cave-temples are also notable for the deeply carved images of Shiva and Vishnu. The Hindu cave at the nearby site of Aihole continues the rock-cut traditions in the Chalukya country and shows evidence of stylistic advances in the slenderness of the columns and the variety of images employed.

The Hindu cave-temples at Ellora, Elephanta and Salsette in the western Deccan form an independent group, though distinct stylistic contacts with northern temple architecture are to be detected in column and doorway designs. The chief interest in these excavations, however, is in the scale of their architectural and sculptural components, which achieves monumentality in carved techniques of the greatest sensitivity. The dating of these temples is not at all clear, but they are most likely to belong to the sixth, seventh and eighth centuries, a period marked by political change in which the Kalachuris were succeeded by the Rashtrakutas. The Hindu excavations at Ellora were influenced by the artistic traditions already established at that site under Buddhist patronage. The Rameshvara cave-temple is one of the earliest of the Hindu series and comprises a columned hall with an ambulatory passageway around three sides of the sanctuary. The façade of the temple consists of a portico with columns whose shafts are almost concealed by a balcony wall, leaving only the central bay open to function as a doorway. The capitals of the columns employ the northern pot motif and have projecting female figures as brackets.

The next stage of the rock-cut phase is represented by the magnificent Dumar Lena cave at Ellora and the two caves on Elephanta and Salsette islands off the western Indian coast. The plans of these temples detach the sanctuary from the rear wall, positioning it in the middle of the columned hall (Fig. 43). There is also the innovation of arranging the interior spaces in a cruciform manner with access from the front and the sides so that multiple axes are created. Additional artificial courtyards are excavated to provide side entrances which, at Elephanta, are provided with subsidiary shrines. Characteristic of these caves is their lack of external façade, access

43 *Opposite top* Plan of the Shiva cave-temple, Elephanta, sixth century; the sanctuary is positioned within and detached from the walls of the columned hall, which are provided with large-scale sculptures dominating the axes of the plan

44 *Opposite bottom* Interior of Shiva cave-temple, Elephanta, showing sanctuary with door-guardians (*dvarapalas*)

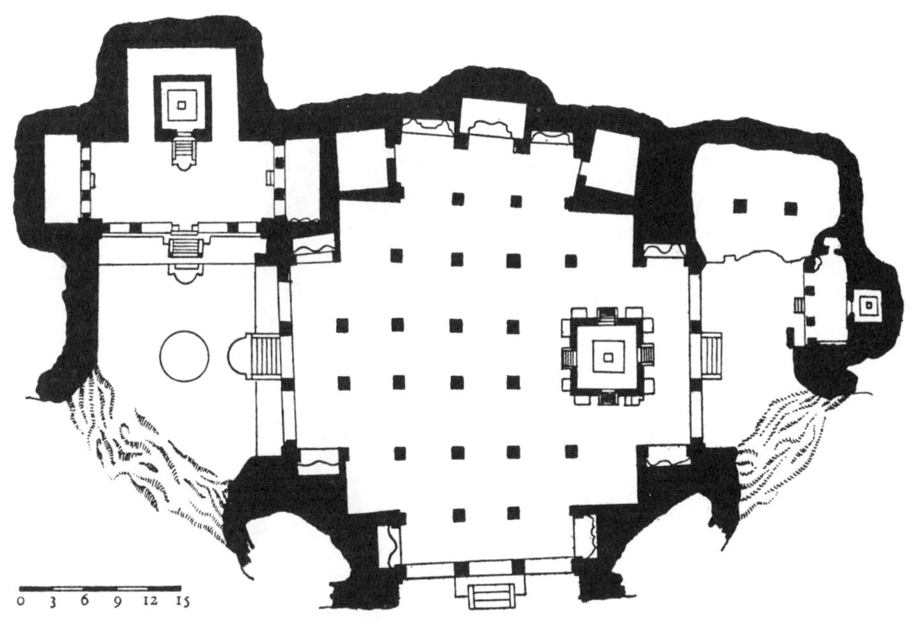
0 3 6 9 12 15

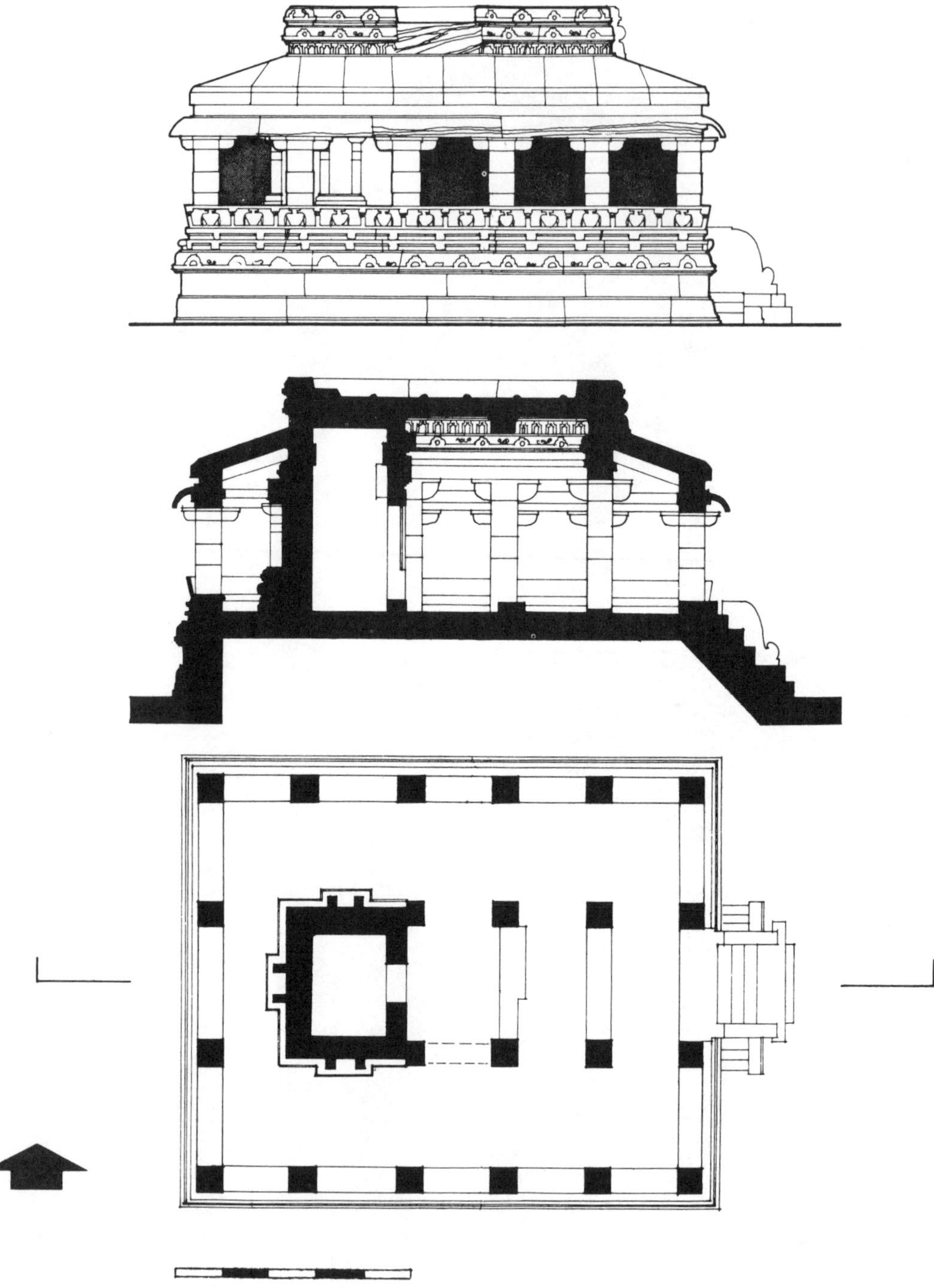

45 Gauda temple, Aihole, seventh century: a unique example of a sanctuary within an open columned porch

being by a simple flight of steps sometimes guarded by lions, and the fluted cushion capitals of their massive interior columns. The square sanctuaries are entered by doorways on all four sides, each flanked by door guardians (Fig. 44); inside are rock-cut Shiva *lingas*. The Elephanta cave introduces the device of a major panel of sculpture—that of Shiva with three heads in the form of the Great Lord, Mahesha—aligned along the principal axis of the cave, providing a focal point for the interior. In order that this composition might have maximum visual impact the sanctuary is moved into the side aisle. Other deeply carved sculptural panels are devoted to scenes from the mythology of Shiva.

Originally a Buddhist monastic excavation, the Dashavatara cave-temple at Ellora was converted into a Hindu shrine under Rashtrakuta patronage in the eighth century. The temple is approached through a rock-cut entrance which opens onto a large and irregularly shaped courtyard with a detached pavilion at its centre, probably intended to house an image of Shiva's mount, Nandi. This pavilion is raised on a moulded plinth and has niches on its outer walls provided with pediments with horseshoe-shaped arches which interlock to form a continuous design. Pierced stone windows are also utilized. The façade of the temple itself is a double-storeyed colonnade, the shafts of the pillars being carved with pot and foliage motifs. The interior of the temple consists of two superimposed columned halls with sculptural panels carved into the rear walls.

The northern style under the Early Chalukyas (seventh to eighth centuries)

Though starting in the middle of the sixth century as a rather localized dynasty, by the beginning of the following century the Chalukyas had rapidly brought about a degree of unification of a large territory of the Deccan that was to continue until their conquest by the Rashtrakutas in the middle of the eighth century. The great fascination of the temples erected under this dynasty at the sites of Badami, Aihole, Pattadakal, Mahakuteshvara and Alampur is that they display a meeting and fragmentation of different temple styles and the creation of local variants. Here is found a preference for open porch-like structures, the use of balcony-slabs with inclined outer surfaces, and the carving of attendant figures and auspicious motifs on the outer columns of the porch. Eventually these features were to become part of both the northern and the southern stylistic repertoires. The dating of these Early Chalukya temples is mainly confined to the seventh and early eighth centuries.

At Aihole some stages in the development of the northern temple style are to be seen which are not found in examples from other parts of India. The Gaudar temple (Fig. 45) is probably a stone copy of an early timber building type. It consists of an open columned structure with the sanctuary positioned at the western end, creating an ambulatory passageway on three sides with a hall to the east. The temple is elevated on a high plinth with a flight of access stairs. The roof-slabs over the central three bays are raised and horizontal while those on four sides are sloping. There is no superstructure, merely a parapet, possibly reflecting a southern stylistic influence. The doorway to the shrine and its outer niches are of the typical northern scheme. The lintel above the opening has horseshoe arched motifs framing miniature icons of the goddess to whom the temple is dedicated, together with her attendants. Also at Aihole is the Chikki temple which repeats this basic architectural formula but replaces the open porch with solid walls in which large pierced stone screens are set, admitting light to the passageway.

Another temple type much in evidence at Aihole combines the sanctuary, columned hall and open porch as three separate elements, clearly articulated on the exterior elevation. In the Huchchappayya temple (Fig. 46) the sanctuary is elevated on a plinth with niches in the centre of the walls on three sides. The brackets of pilasters support a curved cornice which runs around the unadorned walls of the sanctuary and hall. Above the sanctuary rises the superstructure which continues the niche projections beneath, divided into nine horizontal layers decorated with horseshoe arches, in both their complete and their split forms. These layers are combined in three

46 Huchchappayya temple, Aihole, eighth century, showing a clear demarcation of sanctuary with superstructure, hall, and porch

47 Jambulinga temple, Pattadakal, eighth century: an early example of the fully evolved northern superstructure

groups of three mouldings, each group terminated by a ribbed fruit motif, which appears at the corners. The whole was originally capped by a large ribbed element on a circular shaft. Of interest is the projection on the east face of the superstructure, created by a separate stone slab carved in the semblance of a partly circular arch framing an image of Shiva. The doorway to the shrine introduces mouldings from the superstructure as a decoration rising above the lintel. The hall of the temple is of the triple aisle system employing both horizontal and sloping roof-slabs supported on beams carved with animal brackets and other motifs. The undersides of the original horizontal roof-slabs had ceiling panels of Shiva, Brahma and Vishnu; these have now been removed.

A number of modest temples at Aihole, Pattadakal and Mahakuteshvara

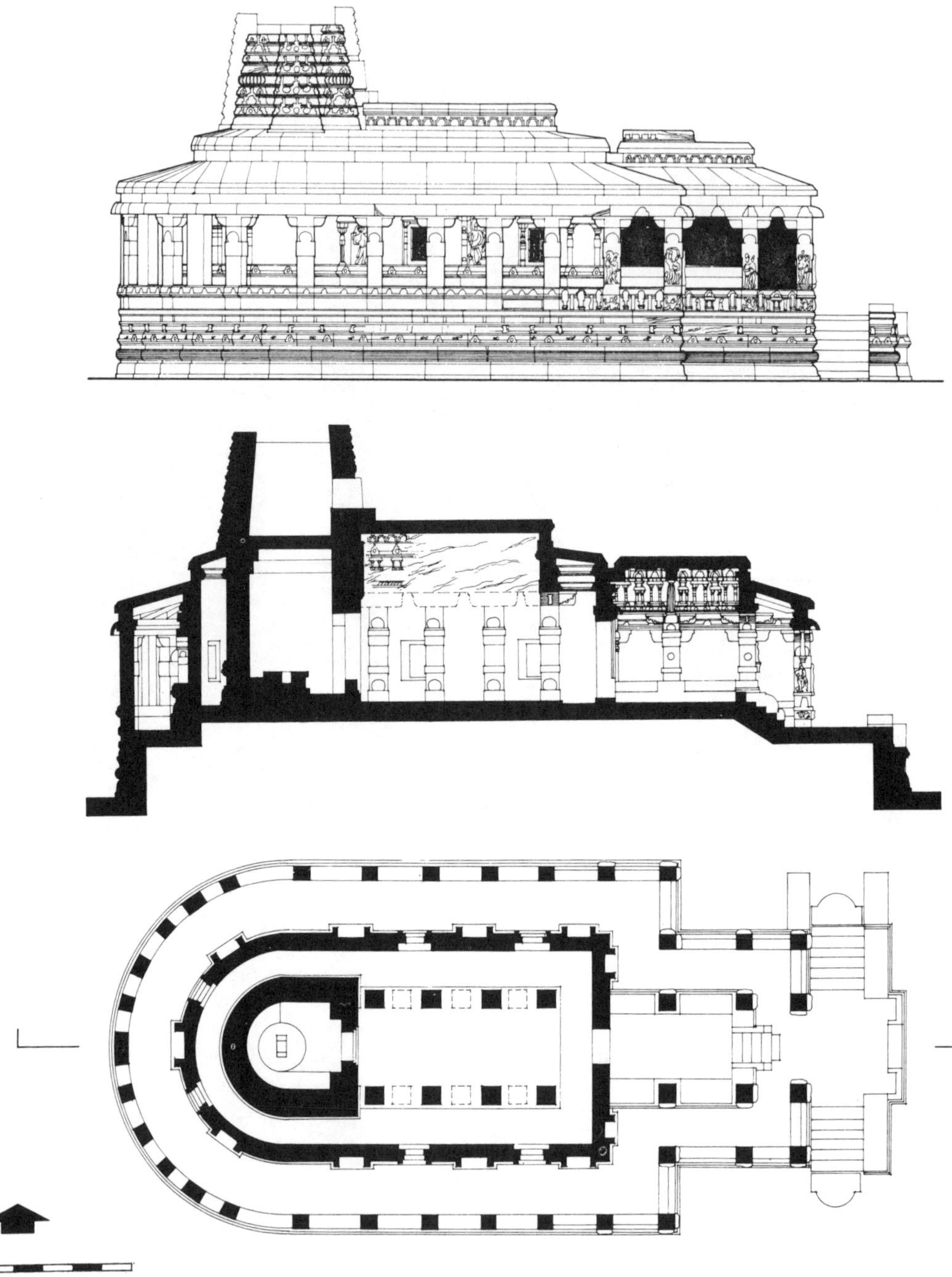

48 Durga temple, Aihole, eighth century: the semi-circular-ended plan is rare in structural architecture, deriving from rock-cut Buddhist sanctuaries

present a reduced version of the Huchchappayya temple type—here a square sanctuary adjoins a small hall or open porch whose roof-slabs are supported on four columns (Fig. 47). In the treatment of the outer walls of the sanctuary, its superstructure and its doorway, these temples are very much alike. However there are innovations, such as in the Pattadakal Kadasiddheshvara temple where the niches on the outer walls are surmounted by pediments created from interlocking horseshoe arched motifs. Similar niche pediments are found on the hybrid Papanatha temple at Pattadakal. This feature is one of the common characteristics of the developed northern temple style.

The celebrated Durga temple at Aihole is one of the finest Early Chalukya buildings, and its apsidal-ended plan is unique in the series (Fig. 48). The temple is laid out so that its partly circular sanctuary is surrounded by an ambulatory passageway, with a columned hall to the east entered by a small porch. This complete temple scheme is set within an open colonnade with balcony seating, which forms an outer passageway. Niches with carved panels and pierced stone screens are provided along the passageway. The temple is elevated on a high moulded plinth, and the outer faces of the columns are carved with sculptures which also extend into the porch. The doorways and ceiling panels of the interior of the temple are finely carved, the latter being in the form of flying celestial couples. Sloping stone slabs in two tiers roof the temple; at the western end is the curious juxtaposition of a square northern superstructure, now partly ruined.

Interesting local variants are found in the monuments at Aihole, especially the Ladkhan (Fig. 31) and Kontgudi temples. These examples have their square and rectangular plans combined with open porch-like portions. Against the back walls of their columned halls are placed small sanctuaries. The Ladkhan temple presents a square hall roofed by a double tier of inclined slabs whose joints are protected by thin stone strips in imitation of wooden logs. Above the central bay are horizontal roof-slabs which support a small upper shrine. The temple is elevated on a plinth and its outer walls are provided with pilasters in the southern manner. Large pierced stone screens light the interior, and the wall is capped by an overhanging eave moulding. The porch leads from the main hall of the temple and is furnished with balcony-slabs and carved columns.

Moving eastwards into the Andhra country, the Chalukya empire established an independent line of rulers early in the seventh century; these were the Eastern Chalukyas. The main centre of their building activity was at Alampur, where nine temples were erected, but there is also a ruined temple at Pattadakal, the Galaganatha, which was probably built by craftsmen from the Eastern Chalukya region (Figs 37, 49). The Svarga Brahma temple at Alampur (Fig. 25) is typical of the group and dates from the end of the seventh century. The sanctuary is enclosed in a rectangle of walls so as to create an ambulatory passageway on three sides and a hall to the east. Porches shelter the entrance to the temple and the pierced stone windows in the passageway walls. The temple is elevated on a moulded

plinth and the walls have a number of projecting niches surmounted by triangular pediments composed of horseshoe arched forms. Stone windows separate the niches and flying attendant figures appear at either side. The niches around the temple house a unique series of images of the guardians of the eight directions of the universe, aligned so that each deity faces towards the direction over which he exercises control. The walls are capped by a simple cornice which supports the bevelled ends of the sloping roof-slabs. The superstructure which rises from the walls of the sanctuary displays a stylistic advance on those of the temples at the other Early Chalukya sites—the outer bands are composed of four groups of mouldings capped by ribbed fruit motifs; the central band has a continuous rising series of arched motifs which interlock to create a mesh design, and the arched projection on the east face of the superstructure is enlarged.

The northern style under the Kalingas and Eastern Gangas (eighth to thirteenth centuries)

The history of Orissa involves the careers of several ruling dynasties, of which the Kalingas and Eastern Gangas were the most prominent. A measure of their political independence is seen in the local architectural and plastic idiom that was developed under their patronage. The Orissan monuments display a coherent stylistic evolution, beginning with modest early examples at Bhubaneshwar and reaching its climax in the ambitious large-scale temple projects at Konarak and Puri. Among the chief characteristics of the Orissan temple style is the emphasis on the horizontal courses employed in the superstructure of the sanctuary and roof of the adjoining hall; these consist of chamfered stone layers between which are deep recesses. Characteristic also is the contrast between the vertical profile of the superstructure, curving only at the very top, and the pyramid-like arrangement of the hall roof.

One of the earliest examples of the Bhubaneshwar group is the eighth-century Parashurameshvara temple, consisting of a square sanctuary to which was later added a columned hall with remarkable pierced stone windows (Fig. 50). The sanctuary has its outer walls provided with projecting central niches flanked by smaller ones at either side. The superstructure has three vertical bands framing two recesses, and rises in a number of layers created by horizontal mouldings decorated with arched forms whose interiors have carved figures and faces. Ribbed fruit motifs at either side divide the superstructure into 'storeys' and, in an enlarged and flattened form, crown the tower with a pot finial above. Many of these elements are taken beneath the cornice to decorate the niches on the walls. On the east face of the tower is an enlarged arch upon a split pair of arches the interiors

49 *Left* Galaganatha temple, Pattadakal, eighth century. The ruined state of this building displays its construction—walls and tower are composed of slabs of stone supporting inclined roof slabs

50 Pierced stone window with dancers and musicians, Parashurameshvara temple, Bhubaneshwar, eighth century

of which are carved with scenes from the mythology of Shiva.

A development of the Orissan style may be observed in the Vaital Deul temple, also at Bhubaneshwar, probably belonging to the ninth century (Fig. 51). Here the sanctuary is rectangular and is positioned on a transverse axis to the adjoining hall. The roof is unusual in the Orissan series—its end elevation presents a large horseshoe arch supported on a pair of split trilobe arches, and the long elevation is barrel vaulted. The walls of the sanctuary are divided rhythmically into projections with carved panels which ascend into the lower parts of the superstructure. The rectangular hall with sloping roof-slabs has miniature shrines with small superstructure forms positioned at the four corners. This latter feature relates the Vaital Deul to the Mukhalingeshvara temple at Mukhalinga, a somewhat earlier building, whose superstructure is simplified into horizontal layers, anticipating later stylistic developments.

In the ninth century Mukteshvara temple at Bhubaneshwar the Orissan style achieves a balance between detailed carved surface decoration and the massed outline of the temple (Fig. 52). Large pierced stone windows flanked by projecting niches are introduced into the walls of the square hall, above which rise designs created by meshes of arched forms that are also applied to the sanctuary walls and superstructure. The roof of the hall is divided into a number of horizontal layers with a pyramidal profile surmounted by a pot finial. The temple is placed within enclosure walls and is approached through a corbelled arch supported on massive pillars. The decorative scheme of the Mukteshvara temple employs both figural and animal motifs, as well as miniature reproductions of the main forms of the building itself, particularly the superstructure.

51 Vaital Deul temple, Bhubaneshwar, ninth century, showing elaborate arched decoration of the tower framing images of the gods worshipped within

52 Mukteshvara temple, Bhubaneshwar, ninth century: clearly divided into sanctuary and hall whose roof forms employ in different ways horizontal layers of deeply undercut mouldings

Further stylistic advances may be detected in the early eleventh-century Lingaraja temple at Bhubaneshwar (Fig. 53): the outer walls of the hall are here divided by a horizontal moulding into two registers, as are the tiers of the hall roof which is surmounted by an inverted bell-shaped fluted form. The superstructure is dominated by the horizontal stratifications but also utilizes miniature reproductions of itself, one above the other, to create vertical bands flanking the central projections on each side. The latter have pronounced arches with projecting mythical animals as gargoyles; beneath the capping roof form are rearing lions and other attendant figures. The Lingaraja temple was enlarged by the addition of two more halls along the principal axis of the temple to create a sequence of successive interior

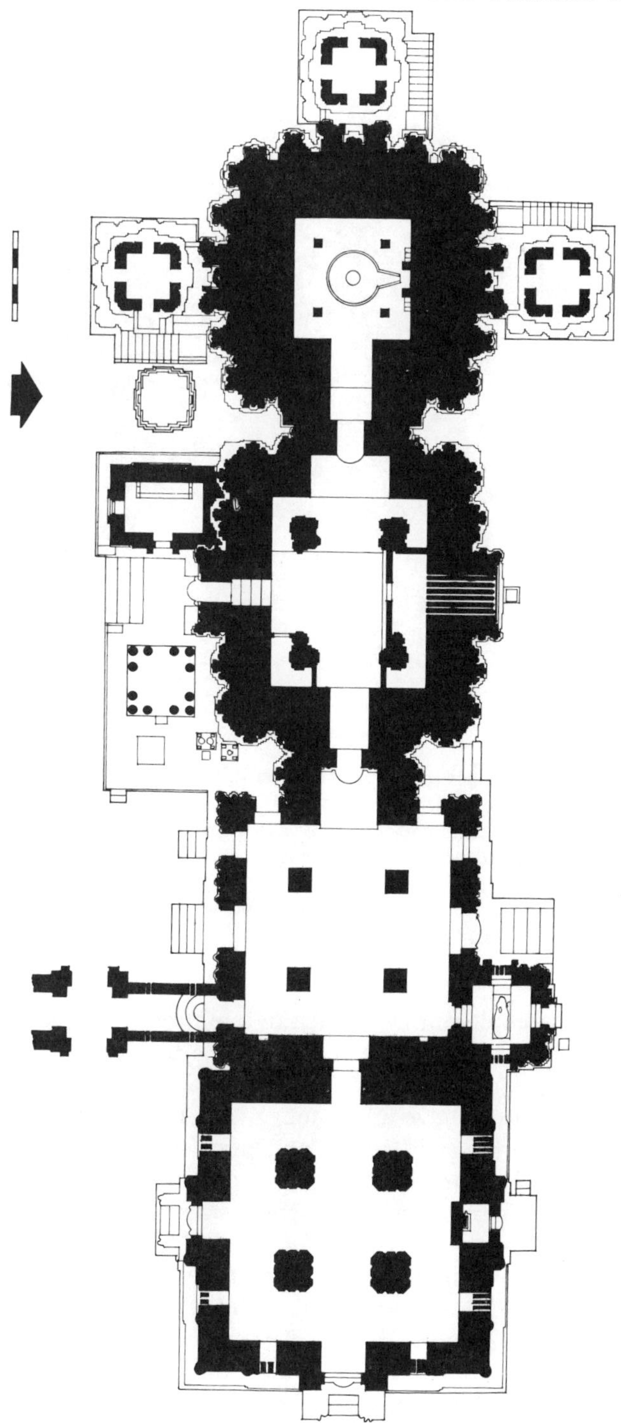

53 Plan of the Lingaraja temple, Bhubaneshwar, eleventh century: a sequence of columned halls leads to the enclosed sanctuary

54 *Above* Detail of the exterior of the Rajarani temple, Bhubaneshwar, eleventh century: accessory divinities flank the central niche which once housed an image of the deity to whom the temple was dedicated

55 *Opposite top* Wheel from the chariot of the Sun god, Surya. Plinth of the Surya temple, Konarak, thirteenth century

56 *Opposite bottom* Plinth of the dancing pavilion, Surya temple, Konarak, decorated with female dancers and musicians

spaces that was to be copied in later Orissan temples. An alternative stylistic development at Bhubaneshwar is seen in the Rajarani temple (Figs 15, 54), possibly completed some time before the Lingaraja. The superstructure of the Rajarani temple rises above a sanctuary with multiple projections. The resulting profile of the tower is bulky, and the horizontal layers are interrupted by miniature versions of the tower applied in clusters around the principal shaft. Of particular interest are the carvings of the guardians of the eight directions of space.

Doubtless, the climax of the Orissan stylistic movement is the Surya temple at Konarak which presents a magnificent architectural ensemble even in its present ruined state. The temple was completed in the middle of the thirteenth century, and was surrounded by enclosure walls with sub-shrines at the corners. The best-preserved part of the temple is the richly carved plinth provided with twelve pairs of wheels and horses, identifying the temple with the chariot of the sun god (Fig. 55). There are also carvings of a multitude

of attendant figures, especially musicians and amorous couples depicted in a variety of sexual postures. In its architectural features the Surya temple shows a continuation of the Orissan style: the roof of the hall has three storeys with free-standing female musicians in the recesses. In front of the temple is a detached columned hall, presumably for music and dancing according to the carved figures depicted on the plinth and pillars (Fig. 56). The Surya temple displays an overall exuberance of both architectural and sculptural forms in which the richness of carved surfaces plays a dominating part. Thereafter, a stylistic decline sets in and later Orissan temples imitate earlier architectural forms without the accompanying rich surface treatment. This is well illustrated in the Jagannatha temple at Puri.

The northern style under the Pratiharas and Chandellas (eighth to eleventh centuries)

Much of central northern India from the eighth century onwards was under the influence of the Pratihara rulers, who erected many small temples at various sites. Most of these structures incorporate the characteristic northern stylistic features—square sanctuary with projecting niches, carved doorway and tower with curved profile, surmounting ribbed motif and arched projection—not unlike similar Early Chalukya temples. By the ninth century, however, distinct stylistic innovations appeared, as may be observed in the Telika Mandir at Gwalior (Fig. 57). This temple has an unusual rectangular sanctuary above which rises the superstructure in a massive barrel vault. The end elevations of the temple present a complex series of interlocking horseshoe arched motifs at different scales, which extend into the horizontal divisions of the tower and function as pediments above the niches and doorways. Over the next few centuries, temples at Gwalior were to exhibit unusual features—especially in their open multi-tiered halls (Fig. 58).

From the middle of the tenth century, Pratihara rule was replaced by the Chandella kingdom which dominated much of central India for the following two hundred years. At Khajuraho, one of its capital cities, over thirty stone temples survive which span the period of Chandella rule, providing evidence of a distinctive and coherent architectural movement. The Khajuraho temples mark the culmination of the northern style in its central Indian expression and reveal clearly defined characteristics in both plan and vertical elevation. Furthermore, the stylistic evolution of the Khajuraho temples attests to the inventiveness of local architectural traditions, which aimed at achieving increasingly complex effects of outer elevational appearance in which the rhythmic modelling of building masses dissolved the barriers between architectural and sculptural forms.

The Khajuraho temples are each elevated on a high terrace providing an ambulatory around the temple, and in some examples, such as the Lakshmana

57 *Opposite top* Telika Mandir temple, Gwalior, ninth century: the upper portions recently restored

58 *Opposite bottom* Sasbahu temple, Gwalior, eleventh century

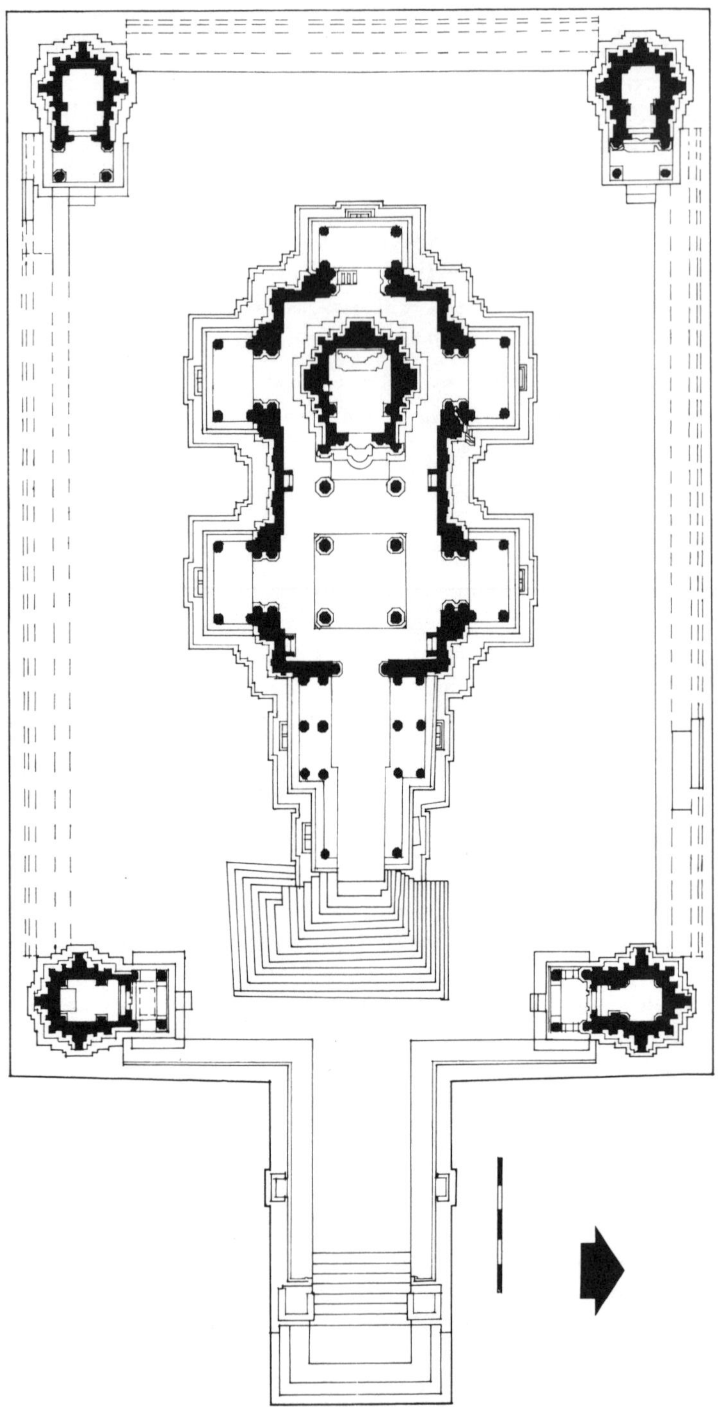

59 Plan of the Lakshmana temple, Khajuraho, tenth century: the principal sanctuary is surrounded by four small shrines, the whole being elevated

60 Musicians from a temple plinth, Khajuraho, tenth century

temple, subsidiary shrines are introduced at the four corners of the platform, rendering the structure a five-shrined complex (*panchayatana*) (Fig. 59). The essential elements of the temple, connected internally on an east-west axis, consist of an entrance porch, hall, vestibule and sanctuary. The latter is usually surrounded on three sides by an ambulatory passageway, and open balconies admit light to the hall and passageway. There are some examples of detached pavilions housing images of the vehicles of the gods to whom the temples are dedicated.

The lower part of the typical Khajuraho temple is deeply moulded into a high plinth, sometimes furnished with horizontal narrative friezes or attendant figures (Fig. 21); also miniature niches for subsidiary images. Above the plinth, and in continuation of its complex outline, rise the walls of the temple, mostly divided into two or more registers by horizontal mouldings. Each of the projections and recesses of the walls is deeply carved with cult images, attendant figures, auspicious couples posed in attitudes of sexual exhibitionism, and rearing animals (Figs 30, 61). The walls are broken by the voids of the balconies, whose lower portions have angled seating-slabs; the outspread decoration is introduced at the principal entrance to the temple where brackets are carved in the semblance of aquatic monsters and garlands.

Above rises the complex roof scheme of the temple, creating the distinctive

61 *Left* Royal couple from temple at Khajuraho, eleventh century
62 *Above* Vishvanatha temple, Khajuraho, eleventh century

silhouette of the temple masses for which Khajuraho is celebrated. Early examples display a single tower with a curved outline surmounted by a ribbed fruit motif and pot finial; the surfaces have a number of projecting bands and are divided into 'storeys' by ribbed motifs. The beginnings of stylistic evolution are seen in the tenth century Lakshmana temple, where a reproduction of the main form of the tower is introduced onto the middle of each side of the principal shaft; the projection on the front face of the tower is in the form of an elaborate niche framing an icon of the god within the temple. Horseshoe arched forms are interwoven to create mesh designs which are everywhere employed. In the Vishvanatha and Kandariya Mahadeva temples erected in the eleventh century the principal shaft of the superstructure is almost completely obscured by a clustering group of miniature towers which grow in number as they descend, providing a summit for each of the projections of the walls beneath. The balconies are

63 Ambulatory passageway within the Vishvanatha temple, Khajuraho, lit by open porches

surmounted by niches which are identical to that projecting from the superstructure and include free-standing mythical animals. The roofs of the halls and porches consist of pyramidal arrangements of horizontal mouldings separated by deep recesses and surmounted by pot finials. The profiles of the temples are dramatically devised, ascending towards the summit of the superstructure above the sanctuary to provide a climax to the temple mass (Fig. 62).

The interiors of the Khajuraho temples are characterized by their tall slender columns with brackets of projecting imps and auspicious females supporting beams decorated with foliage designs. The chief interest is provided by the dome-like ceiling above the central spaces of the porches and halls; these are frequently sculptured with lobe-like cusps rising in diminishing circles or ellipses to a pendant lotus bud. The doorway to the sanctuary is elaborately carved in the characteristic northern manner, and the images in niches in the outer walls are illuminated by a subtle lighting from the open balconies (Fig. 63).

The northern style under the Maitrakas and Solankis (eighth to thirteenth centuries)

The earliest temples of Gujarat are attributed to the Maitraka rulers who gained control of the region in the seventh century. The Maitraka temples are small buildings of simple plan, with superstructures created by a series of diminishing stepped mouldings decorated with bold horseshoe arched 'windows'. A number of temples of this class are known at various sites throughout Gujarat. The temples at Roda, dating from the eighth and ninth centuries, are typical of another group of monuments in Gujarat executed in the northern stylistic formula. These temples have square sanctuaries provided with single or triple projections and adjoin a small porch. In the more developed examples, horizontal bands divide the walls into two registers and there is the utilization of ornamental friezes of garlands and bells. The towers of these temples are mostly covered with the characteristic mesh design with a large and flattened ribbed motif above. The niche on the front of the tower is greatly projected in the Roda temples, its triangular shape being created from a manipulation of arched forms.

Under the Solanki kings who succeeded the Maitrakas early in the eleventh century, Gujarat developed a distinctive and prolific regional architectural style. One of the earliest temples to be built in the new style was the Surya temple at Modhera, the capital of the Solanki empire. Now in a ruined state, the temple consists of two structures and an artificial tank aligned along an east-west axis (Fig. 64). The columned hall is arranged with its long side transversely disposed towards the principal orientation of the temple complex, its plan spreading outwards in a number of projecting bays. Here are found many of the characteristic features of the Solanki version of the northern temple style. Balcony-slabs of the hall are divided into panels carved with attendant figures above which rise the columns with vase and foliage motifs at their bases. The capitals of these columns are

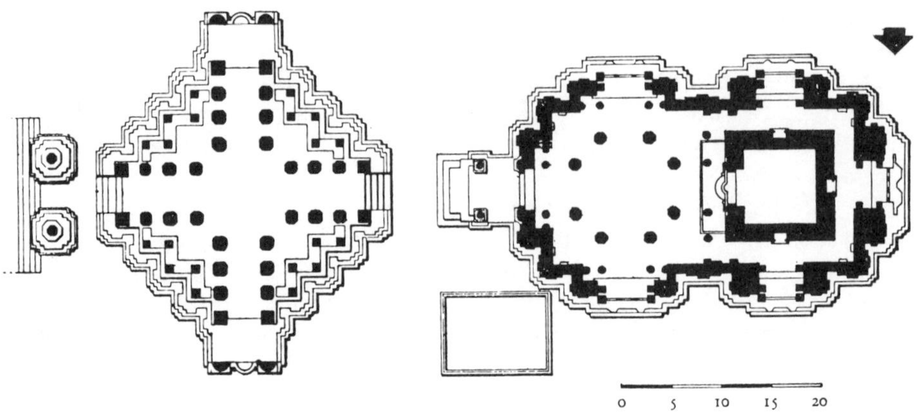

64 Plan of Surya temple, Modhera, eleventh century: the sanctuary (*right*) is detached from the open columned hall, outside which steps lead down to a tank

65 *Opposite* Interior of open columned hall, Surya temple, Modhera: the highly decorated, cusped arches only appear to support the heavy stone beams

diminished, thus emphasizing the brackets fashioned into foliage and animal motifs. The interior columns have their shafts carved with bands of lion masks and mythological scenes. Springing from intermediate capitals halfway up the shafts are open-mouthed aquatic monster brackets supporting curved and cusped arches created by garlands and lotus buds. These appear to hang suspended between the columns framing the entrances to the hall and the central interior space. The outer columns have their brackets supporting an overhanging eave (Fig. 65). The temple itself consists of a hall and sanctuary surrounded on three sides by an ambulatory passageway. Six porches admit light, that to the east functioning as the principal entrance. The superstructure has now completely disappeared. An exquisitely carved and lobed archway leads to the large tank which is provided with numerous flights of steps interspersed with miniature shrines of various sizes.

The temples at other sites in Gujarat, dating from the eleventh century onwards, demonstrate the essential characteristics of the developed Solanki style. Here the sanctuary is no longer surrounded by a passageway, and the outer walls are divided into a number of projections so that the plan approaches that of a circle. The walls of the sanctuary are diminished in elevation and sculptures on each projection are surmounted by triangular pediments of arched motifs. A number of cornices provide the transition to the superstructure, which continues the projections of the walls upwards. The tower is composed of a series of miniature superstructure forms, each decorated with mesh designs and surmounted by ribbed motifs, arranged in horizontal layers which diminish as they ascend, eventually to reveal the central shaft of the principal tower. The chief features of the columned hall

66 Harihara temple, Osian, ninth century: the niches of the sanctuary are copied, complete with images, on the plinth

are intricately carved columns and brackets which support a complex beam system upon which rise carved dome-like ceilings characteristic of temple architecture in Gujarat.

For the climax of the Solanki temple style in the thirteenth century and later, it is necessary to turn to the marble Jain temples of Gujarat and Rajasthan, many of which are concentrated on sacred hill sites such as at Mount Abu.

The northern style in Rajasthan (eighth to twelfth centuries)

The monuments at Osian are early examples of the regional stylistic variation that developed in Rajasthan from the eighth century onwards (Fig. 66). The superstructures of the temples at this site display a typical northern stylistic treatment, and are divided into a number of bands which continue the projections of the walls beneath. The central bands are usually decorated with meshes of arched motifs, while the outer bands have the simpler forms of the arch combined with ribbed fruit motifs. The walls of the sanctuary hold sculptures flanked by pilasters surmounted by triangular pediments created from interlocking arched forms. A double cornice moulding containing a horizontal frieze of relief sculpture functions as a transition from the sanctuary walls to the superstructure above. A stylistic evolution within the Osian group is seen in the increasingly elaborate porches that adjoin the sanctuaries, the columns of which have their bases and capitals carved with pot and foliage designs, and their brackets with fluted palm-leaf motifs. In the more ambitious projects which belong to the later phases at Osian in the ninth and tenth centuries, the temples are combined into groups and are elevated upon raised platforms with moulded plinths and sculptured friezes.

Further stylistic developments are found at other sites in Rajasthan, such as Chitorgarh and Badoli, built during the ninth and tenth centuries. Here there is a further elaboration of the tower with strongly demarcated vertical bands covered with mesh designs. The projection on the front of the superstructure, which is supported on the adjoining porch roof, has increased in complexity. The most representative example of late tenth and eleventh century Rajasthani temple architecture is the group of temples at Kiradu which continues the stylistic evolution and introduces the clustered type of tower. From the twelfth century onwards the northern style in Rajasthan lost its individuality and eventually merged with the Solanki style as regions in Rajasthan came under the political and cultural influence of Gujarat.

Kashmir and other Himalayan valleys (eighth century to modern period)

The most northerly extension of Hindu architecture is marked by the lower valleys of the Himalayas. The varying forms of the Himalayan temples reflect the independent histories of these regions and their isolated stylistic developments. Though brick building in Kashmir goes back to the centuries before Christ when the valley was dominated by Buddhism, the earliest stone Hindu temples are traced only to the reign of Lalitaditya, who ruled Kashmir in the eighth century. It was under his patronage that the great Surya temple at Martand was constructed. This large-scale project consists of a rectangular sanctuary with deep niches on three sides and an entrance to the east formed by a small vestibule, within a colonnaded enclosure entered by a gateway. Though now greatly ruined, the monumental ensemble at Martand displays typical features of the architectural style developed in Kashmir. Prominent among these is the enlarged trilobe arch set in a gable roof which surmounts the niches and doorways to the sanctuary and probably originally the gateway as well. This trilobe arch is created entirely by horizontal corbelled grey sandstone slabs and, together with the moulded plinths and cornices of the walls, the shallow pilasters and the colonnade, shows distinct influences from Hellenistic architecture. Typical among these

67 Shiva temple, Pandrethan, ninth or tenth century. The trilobe arch which frames the doorway is characteristic of the Kashmir style

influences are the Corinthian columns and torus mouldings, as well as the egg and dart motifs. The sequel to the Martand temple is seen in the ruins of the ninth-century Vishnu temple at Avantesvami, also in the Kashmir valley.

The typical temple style of Kashmir and its relation to timber architectural forms is well illustrated in the small Shiva temple at Pandrethan, possibly belonging to the ninth or tenth century (Figs 34, 67). Here a square sanctuary has entrances on all four sides, each provided with a portico created by a triangular gable roof in which a trilobe arch frames the opening. The roof above is sloping and is divided into two tiers with miniature horseshoe-headed 'windows'. As at Martand, there are vestiges of Hellenistic influences. Of great interest in this small temple is the ceiling, with lotus designs and flying attendant figures; the pattern of rotating and diminishing squares reflects the impact of a structural system in which diagonal beams are employed in order to reduce the span.

Almost no stone temples are found in the other Himalayan valleys of Kulu, Kangra and Chamba, and here timber and brick building traditions dominate temple forms. The sloping and gabled roofs which are preserved only in stone in the temples of Kashmir appear here in their original wooden context. The temples of these valleys are small in scale, and their tiers of sloping roofs characteristically diminish as they ascend. Stone is sometimes retained for the doorways and walls of the shrine, and stylistic contacts with the northern style are found in the decoration of the door-frames. In the carving of the timber columns and beams the most refined craftsmanship is displayed and there is a preference for pot and foliage capitals and lotus designs. At Masrur in Kangra, a remarkable multi-towered temple was excavated into a natural escarpment in the ninth century or later. The nine superstructures which constitute this temple rise above a number of shrines arranged in a row. The lower parts of the walls are carved into large niches framed by recessed and decorated bands. The curved forms of the towers have the characteristic northern features of mesh designs as well as clusters of miniature reproductions of the principal tower.

68 Dattatreya temple, Bhadgaon, seventeenth or eighteenth century: tiled roofs are supported by carved timber struts

69 Doorway of shrine near the Shiva temple, Pashupathinath, nineteenth century: further shrines are visible through the doorway

Nepal (seventeenth century to modern period)

No ancient Hindu temples have been preserved in Nepal, though isolated architectural and sculptural fragments from the early centuries of Hindu influence attest to the long artistic tradition going back to Gupta times. In the seventeenth and eighteenth centuries the Kathmandu valley was ruled by a local dynasty, the Malla kings, and under their influence civic complexes at Kathmandu, Patan and Bhadgaon were constructed. In the central spaces of these towns, the *durbar* squares, palaces were grouped together with Hindu temples. Some of these temples were constructed in stone to imitate the northern curved superstructure forms. Of interest in these urban ensembles are the stone columns upon which were elevated gilded images of the Malla kings (Fig. 18) or of accessory sacred images such as Garuda, depicted in devotional attitudes and aligned on an axis with the entrance to the temples with which they are associated.

The examples of Himalayan tiered wooden architecture found in the temples of the Kathmandu valley are unique (Fig. 68). The timber construction of these temples employs a central brick core which houses the sanctuary and from which project angled timber struts, supporting the overhanging sloping roofs. These roofs ascend until they reach the inverted-bell-like finial, often gilded. Timber doorways placed in the brick walls, the timber struts, and the interlocking timber screens bear the most refined examples of the art of wood-carving to have been preserved in the subcontinent. The decoration of these timber members incorporates a repertoire of motifs common in the northern style—the pot and foliage design, river goddesses, aquatic monsters, lion masks, and the ever-popular motif of Garuda crushing serpents. Particularly prominent is the demonic mask, which is employed in combination with a wide range of fearful deities (Fig. 69). This emphasis in the sacred art of Nepal upon themes of fear and terror has clear parallels with the Hindu art of South-East Asia.

The southern style under the Pallavas (seventh to eighth centuries)

The architectural growth of the southern Indian temple is well ordered and linear in its evolution. Temples developed from the earliest known rock-cut efforts of the Pallavas in the seventh century through the great structural efforts of the Chola kings in the eleventh century to the temple-city complexes which reached their greatest expansion under the patronage of the Vijayanaga kings in the sixteenth century.

The reigns of the Pallava kings covered approximately a century and a half, ending towards the middle of the eighth century. During this period the development of Hindu architecture was evidently proceeding at a rapid rate, and there are remains of more than sixty temples excavated under Pallava patronage, together with numerous monolithic and structural temples. There is also evidence of a rapid transition from the rock-cut medium via the monolithic phase to structural temple building.

Early seventh-century rock-cut temples of the Pallava king Mahendra are found at many sites throughout Tamil Nadu, and they constitute the beginnings of the southern phase of rock-cut temple architecture. They each consist of a pillared hall serving as a portico for one or more small sanctuaries cut deeply into the interior wall. The external appearance of these temples presents a façade formed by a row of pillars with plain shafts and curved brackets. The more developed examples are provided with an overhanging eave, sometimes decorated with horseshoe arched 'windows'. The next stage in the evolution of these early cave-temples is found at Mahabalipuram, once the port of the Pallava kingdom. In the ten excavations at this site carried out under the patronage of the ruler Mamalla in the second half of the seventh century, distinct innovations are incorporated: there are the rudimentary beginnings of the parapet, or mouldings which rise above the overhanging eave, and the lower parts of the column shafts are fashioned into heraldic lions, a royal emblem. Elaborate sculptural compositions furnish the otherwise unrelieved interiors of the caves.

The series of monolithic temples known as '*rathas*' (literally, 'chariots') at Mahabalipuram provide a veritable catalogue of the architectonic forms and sacred icons current during the seventh and eighth centuries in southern India. Despite the fact that this monolithic phase was only transitory, the '*rathas*' reveal a true sophistication of craftsmanship and an imaginative elaboration of the southern Indian architectural formula (Fig. 33). Each '*ratha*' presents a different appearance, but there are a number of general features they have in common which define the stylistic elements fundamental to the southern temple style. These elements remain constant throughout the history of the south Indian temple well beyond the Pallava period. The '*rathas*' are each elevated on a moulded plinth above which the walls divide rhythmically into a number of projections and recesses created by pairs of shallow pilasters. Sculptures of deities, semi-divine figures, and royal personalities are set in rectangular niches. Some of the more important images are framed by pairs of pilasters whose brackets do not extend the full height of the wall but carry a pair of aquatic monsters with foliated tails and open jaws. The curved brackets of the wall pilasters and porch columns support an overhanging eave with carved arched 'windows' from which faces occasionally peer. Above rises a series of mouldings culminating in the parapet—perhaps the most distinctive element of the southern architectural style. This is created from a series of ornamental miniature roof forms arranged in rows around the building. These may be square or rectangular in plan and have curved contours suggesting the original timber barrel vaults of which they are stone models. The Arjuna and Dharmaraja '*rathas*' repeat at a higher level the complete wall system—pilastered surface, eave and parapet—on a reduced plan, so that their vertical elevations proceed upwards in a series of receding storeys. These are the earliest instances of the typical southern superstructure. The other '*rathas*' do not have these upper storeys, but all utilize a variety of capping curved roof forms that are either square, rectangular, octagonal, or apsidal-ended.

70 Detail from open-air relief carving—'Arjuna's penance', Mahabalipuram, seventh century. In a cleft between two large boulders snake gods are carved over which water was made to flow, representing the Ganges descending to earth. To the banks of the Ganges came gods, semi-divine beings, humans and animals. *Left* is a representation of a Vishnu temple in the southern style, before which a sage is seated

Carved on one of the granite boulders at Mahabalipuram is one of the largest bas-relief compositions known in India (Fig. 70). This was probably executed during the reign of Mamalla and is dedicated to the theme of Arjuna's penance, one of the episodes in the *Mahabharata*. Of interest in this carving is the appearance of a model shrine which represents a square structural temple with a curved roof and a four-armed image of Vishnu against the back wall. Seated before the shrine are an ascetic and his pupils. A similar architectural scheme is found in another stone model shrine (Fig. 35).

The importance of the contribution of the Pallava king Rajasimha to the development of south Indian temple architecture in the early eighth century

71 Twin towers of the 'Shore' temple, Mahabalipuram, eighth century

can hardly be overestimated. Under his patronage structural temple building in granite was initiated and the 'Shore' temple at Mahabalipuram, probably the earliest structural Pallava stone building, shows a mastery of the new style (Fig. 71). The temple actually consists of a group of three sanctuaries, two of which are provided with superstructures, set within a complex of minor shrines, open halls, enclosure walls and gateways; much of this complex is now buried in the sand. The oldest part of the temple is a seventh-century image of Vishnu sleeping, cut out of a natural boulder. Only in the following century was this image housed in a small structure, in combination with two other shrines which, judging from the fluted *lingas* placed there and the images carved on their rear walls, were dedicated to Shiva. The 'Shore' temple introduces an ambulatory passageway around the principal shrine and emphasizes the doorway to this shrine by a prominent ornamental barrel vaulted roof form. The outer walls of the shrine and passageways are divided into bays by pilasters whose lower portions are fashioned into rearing lions. The superstructures rise steeply and, as in the

Arjuna and Dharmaraja '*rathas*', proceed in a series of diminutive repetitions of the wall scheme (Fig. 33). Both towers are capped with octagonal roof forms and pot-shaped finials.

The temples built next after the 'Shore' temple are found at Kanchipuram, the ancient capital of the Pallava kingdom. These buildings were executed in a soft sandstone medium, but granite was retained for hard-wearing surfaces such as the floor and steps. The Kailasanatha temple was Rajasimha's masterpiece and, in its original form, consisted of a square sanctuary provided with sub-shrines built into its outer walls, together with a detached open columned hall which was later joined to the sanctuary. Surrounding both is a large enclosure created by a series of minor shrines arranged in rows and dedicated to a whole host of divinities. Each of these is provided with its own miniature hemispherical roof form.

In the Vaikunthaperumal temple at Kanchipuram, which was built some decades after the Kailasanatha in the middle of the eighth century, the Pallava architectural style reaches its most mature expression. Here, the elements found in previous schemes are brought together into a har-

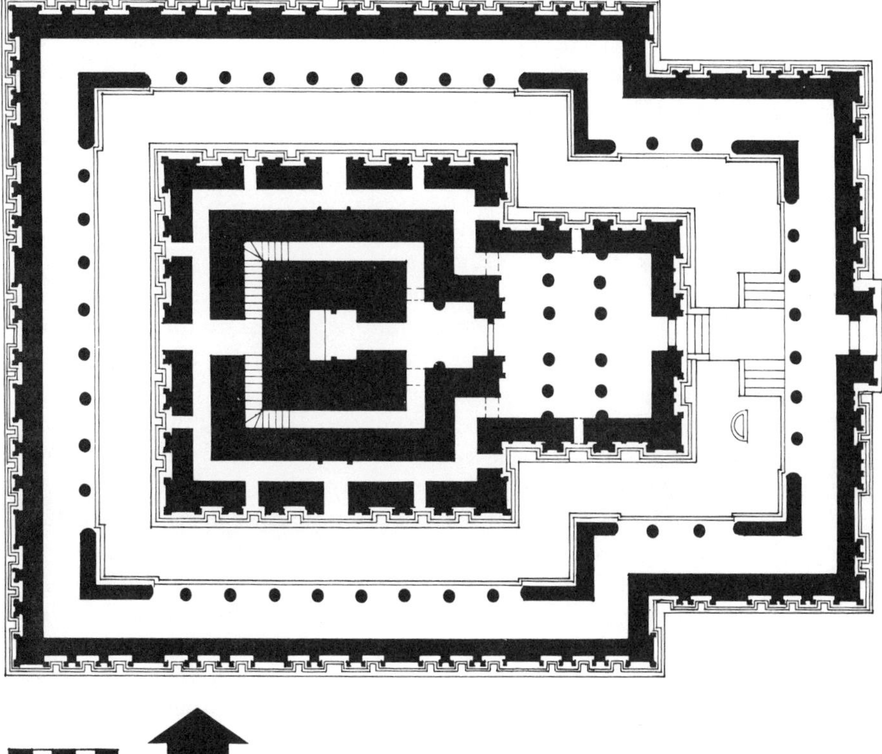

72 Plan of the Vaikunthaperumal temple, Kanchipuram, eighth century: closely co-ordinated ensemble consisting of sanctuary, double passageway, hall, open courtyard and colonnade

monious and economic ensemble (Fig. 72). For the first time in the southern structural temple, the pillared hall comes to adjoin the square sanctuary and its surrounding ambulatory passageways. This is then set within a courtyard whose enclosure walls frame an open portico. Along the internal surface of the outer walls is carved a series of important historical reliefs (Fig. 19). At Kanchipuram the diagnostic features of the south Indian temple style, first apparent in the '*rathas*' at Mahabalipuram, continue to evolve in the increasing complexity of individual elements and their combination.

The southern style under the Early Chalukyas (seventh to eighth centuries)

Temples in the northern style at Badami, Aihole, Pattadakal and Alampur have already been noted, but there is also a significant group of southern styled temples at some of these sites which present a clear and coherent stylistic evolution. Because of the political feuds between the Early Chalukya and the Pallava rulers, whose kingdoms were adjacent, there were considerable stylistic contacts between the architectural productions of the two dynasties.

Probably the earliest extant structural Chalukya monument, and perhaps the earliest southern styled free-standing building to have been preserved, is the Meguti temple at Aihole. This building belongs to the reign of Pulakeshin II during the first third of the seventh century. Though now partly ruined, the temple presents a clear statement of the typical southern stylistic elements in its outer appearance—the moulded plinth, the rhythmic division of the wall into projecting and recessed bays by pairs of pilasters, and the overhanging eave above which rises the parapet. Unfortunately, the superstructure of the Meguti temple is now replaced by a later addition which gives no indication of the original design. In plan, the temple presents a square sanctuary surrounded on all four sides by an ambulatory passageway. To the east is a small columned hall approached by a flight of steps. Elaborations of this scheme are found in the two Shivalaya temples at Badami. The 'Upper' Shivalaya has its sanctuary surrounded by a rectangle of walls so as to create a passageway on three sides and a pillared hall and porch to the east; above the sanctuary rises the superstructure crowned by a large square roof form. The Malegitti Shivalaya has no passageway, the sanctuary merely adjoining a rectangular shaped hall with a porch. The octagonal roof form of the superstructure is contained within four miniature shrines and is supported on a repetition of the wall surface complete with eave and parapet (Fig. 73).

Further developments of these temple types are found in the two examples at the sacred site of Mahakuteshvara dating from the late seventh century. Here the pillared halls are enlarged so as to create a central aisle and double side aisles; the passageway on three sides of the sanctuary is retained. There is also the innovation of a detached structure which houses Nandi, the bull of Shiva to whom both these temples are dedicated. The superstructure repeats the scheme of the Badami Malegitti Shivalaya temple. Character-

73 Malegitti Shivalaya temple, Badami, seventh century: the temple is built of the same red sandstone as that on which it stands

istic of all the Early Chalukya temples are the interior spaces created by raised horizontal roof-slabs over the central aisle of the hall with sloping slabs on three sides. The under-surfaces of the slabs are carved with ceiling panels, and the columns themselves are decorated with a variety of motifs on their shafts, mainly contained within raised bands and circles. Pierced stone windows are employed in the temples, together with narrative relief carvings along the bands of the plinth.

These temples would seem to have been a preparation for the great eighth-century building projects undertaken at Pattadakal, a royal commemorative site, under the patronage of the kings Vijayaditya and his son Vikramaditya II. The Sangameshvara temple is the first of the series and shows a distinct advance on the temples from other Chalukya sites, particularly in the

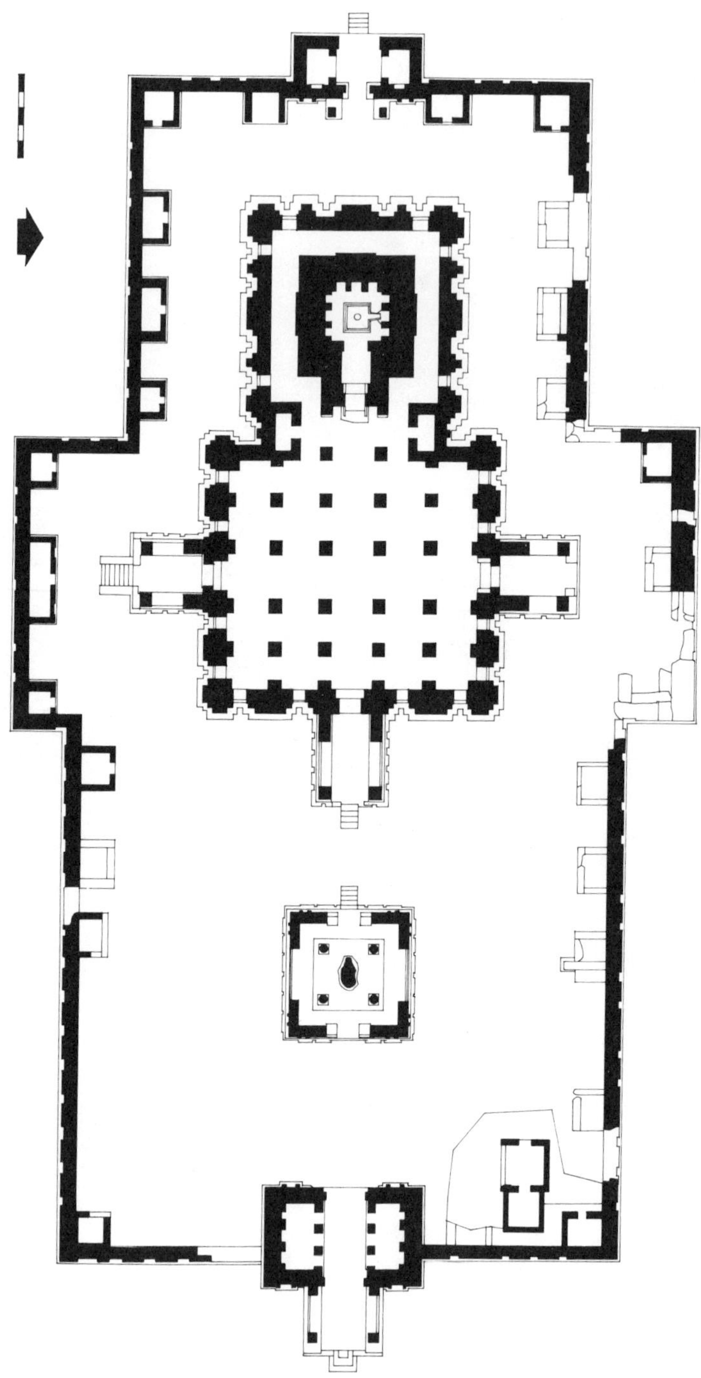

74 Plan of the Virupaksha temple, Pattadakal, eighth century: the outer walls, containing two gateways, enclose the temple to the god and the pavilion for his vehicle

75 Looking across the enclosure wall into the courtyard of the Virupaksha temple, Pattadakal. *Left* is the detached pavilion; *right*, the tower of the adjacent Mallikarjuna temple

enlarged architectural scale and the development of the superstructure which rises in several superimposed layers of diminishing wall systems. The square cell of this temple is surrounded on three sides by a passageway and adjoins a large pillared hall to the east with access by three porches. The Virupaksha temple presents a plan identical to that of the Sangameshvara, but introduces minor shrines within the hall for subsidiary deities (Figs 74, 75). The temple is set within an enclosure with sub-shrines arranged around the walls. In front of the temple is a detached open pavilion housing a Nandi image (Fig. 76). Gateways are positioned in the centres of the east and west walls of the enclosure. Innovations are found in the elaboration of the rhythmic projections of the outer walls of the temple, which achieve emphasis by means of double projections. The number of sculptural panels is greatly increased and virtuoso carving techniques are found in the pierced stone windows (Fig. 77). The interior of the temple has its columns richly furnished with relief carvings which introduce a variety of mythological subjects. The device of ceiling panels is retained and extends also into the porches. The superstructure system rises steeply, the number of storeys is increased and

76 *Above left* Shiva's bull, Nandi, in the pavilion of the Virupaksha temple, Pattadakal; the cloth draped over the bull indicates that it is still in worship
77 *Above right* Pierced stone window, Virupaksha temple, Pattadakal
78 *Opposite top* Papanatha temple, Pattadakal, eighth century
79 *Opposite bottom* Doorway within the Papanatha temple, Pattadakal

the relative size of the square capping roof form is reduced. There is the significant projection on the front of the tower, as a large horseshoe arch framing an image of Shiva dancing. The doorways to the hall and sanctuary are elaborately carved and each frames the opening with a pair of pilasters supporting an overhanging ornamental eave. Aquatic monsters with foliated tails embellish the capitals of these pilasters. Above rises a series of mouldings derived from the upper parts of the outer walls. Some indication of the final evolution of the Early Chalukya architectural style may be seen in the hybrid Papanatha temple, also at Pattadakal. Here the southern elements of pilastered wall with eave and surmounting parapet are combined with northern niche pediments and superstructure (Fig. 78). Richly carved ceiling panels and columns decorate the interior (Figs 4, 79).

The southern style under the Rashtrakutas (eighth to tenth centuries)

Further developments of the southern architectural phase are seen in at least one monument of the Rashtrakutas who, under Dantidurga, wrested the supremacy of the Deccan from the Chalukyas in the middle of the eighth century and held it for the following two hundred years. The monuments produced under Rashtrakuta patronage are mostly rock-cut; their northern styled monuments have already been described.

The Kailasa temple at Ellora, begun under Dantidurga, presents the most dramatic exercise in the rock-cut monolithic medium in India (Fig. 80). Its dimensions alone are remarkable—the courtyard in which the temple stands measures some 100 by 53 metres and the sanctuary itself is over 30 metres high. The temple is a perfect facsimile of a structural building, complete with courtyard, sub-shrines and entrance gateway. It is fashioned out of the sloping hillside by deep trenches which isolated the mass from which the temple was carved. The Kailasa temple shows a further evolution of the southern style that had developed under Early Chalukya patronage at Pattadakal. The temple itself is elevated as an upper storey and consists of a square sanctuary surrounded by an open ambulatory passageway with subsidiary minor shrines. The square pillared hall has central and double side aisles with three balconied porches, one of which provides access by means of an elevated bridge to the Nandi pavilion. The whole is set within a colonnade off which open auxiliary shrines, mostly later additions. An entrance gateway with a barrel vaulted roof form, two free-standing monolithic columns and two elephants complete the ensemble.

The southern characteristic features of moulded base, pilastered wall, overhanging eave and parapet which, when combined in diminishing superimposition, create the superstructure, are all found in the Kailasa temple. But there are variations in the treatment of the walls, which are greatly increased in height and provided with slender pilasters. The scheme of projecting and recessing the wall is mostly abandoned, variety being introduced by the device of creating secondary niches in which pilasters terminate in ornamental pediments of eave and parapet design. Sculptures on the walls are not confined to panels, and the many images and scenes illustrate Epic stories (Fig. 16) and the mythology of Shiva, after whose mountain retreat the temple is named. Innovations are the monumental frieze of elephants which supports the sanctuary, and the rich decoration of the columns, balconies, eaves and parapets. Auxiliary shrines such as the Lankeshvara, belonging to the ninth century and later, demonstrate a further stylistic advance, especially the columns which become overburdened with ornament and squatter in proportion.

80 *Left* Tower of the principal shrine, Kailasa temple, Ellora, eighth century: this temple was cut out of the hillside, downwards, to produce a free-standing building

81 Brihadeshvara temple, Tanjore, eleventh century: the crowning circular roof form is cut from a large single stone mass

82 Detail of the sanctuary of the Brihadeshvara temple, Gangaikondacholapura

The southern style under the Cholas (tenth to eleventh centuries)

By the end of the eighth century the major impulse of Pallava and Chalukya architecture had largely ended, to be followed by a period of dynastic unrest in south India. Towards the end of the ninth century the Cholas emerged as the dominant political force in the area. Preoccupied as these rulers were with the consolidation of their empire, the early centuries of the Chola kingdom saw only the gradual growth of an architectural ideal. This began with modest single storeyed shrines with square or octagonal towers in the manner of late Pallava models. Individual characteristics, such as the multi-faceted column with projecting square capital, indicate the emergence of the new Chola style. The amount of sculpture on the walls of temples increases and friezes of mythical animals or *vyalas* are introduced for the uppermost course of the deeply moulded plinth.

It was under the patronage of Rajaraja at the opening of the eleventh century that the first great Chola building projects were initiated. Temples from this period and the following two centuries express a new sense of imposing power which attests to the considerable concentration of wealth of the Chola kings and the artistic expertise that they promoted. The first of the temples to embody the new monumentalism was the Brihadeshvara temple at Tanjore, completed in about the year 1000 (Fig. 81). This temple is composed of several structures aligned axially—a sanctuary, Nandi pavilion, pillared hall and assembly hall—in the centre of a spacious walled enclosure furnished with sub-shrines. The most important part of this scheme is the sanctuary, whose walls are divided into two storeys by an intermediate eave moulding. The chamber within, housing the image of the god, is located on a level coinciding with the upper storey. In the characteristic southern manner the walls of the Brihadeshvara temple are divided into projections and recesses by pilasters provided with deeply cut sculptures. At the centre of each side of the sanctuary one bay is prominently projected, emphasizing the principal cult icons housed there. Above rise the parapet and superstructure composed of many diminishing storeys which repeat the features of the walls. The whole is capped by an octagonal domed roof form. The tower of this temple is celebrated for its great height—almost 50 metres—and for the subtle tapering profile of the pyramidal mass.

The other great building produced at this time is that at Gangaikondacholapuram, the capital of the Chola empire, erected during the reign of Rajendra I, the successor to Rajaraja (Fig. 82). The temple repeats the basic scheme found at Tanjore, but modifies the bulk of the superstructure so that it rises less steeply, introducing for the first time a very gently concave curved profile. Associated with the sanctuary is an open hall containing over 150 pillars, an early example of the extensive columned halls which were to become such a feature of the south Indian temple.

The later Chola period witnessed a degeneration in architectural modulations recompensed to some extent by an exuberance of ornamental embellishment. The twelfth-century temples at Darasuram and other sites clearly paved the way for the prestigious complexes promoted by the Pandyas and Vijayanagas.

Temple styles of the Hoyshalas and Later Chalukyas (eleventh to fourteenth centuries)

The Hoyshalas and Later Chalukya kings were prominent rulers of the Deccan, and under their patronage distinct architectural styles were evolved. Though these have points of contact with the northern and southern temple styles, there are sufficient distinctive features in the Hoyshala and Later Chalukya temples to justify their independent grouping. One of these features is the obscuring of the outer profile of the building by multiplying the projections of the walls and superstructure; these move restlessly from

83 Keshava temple, Somnathpur, thirteenth century: its three sanctuaries have identical superstructures

one plane to another, relying upon effects of light and shade to lend the building its solidity and shape. Another feature of these temples is the material from which they are mostly built—a greenish-grey chlorite schist. This stone promoted a certain virtuoso style of carving in which great precision of detail was combined with the possibility of deep undercutting.

The evolution of the Hoyshala temple style may be observed in the remarkable trio of twelfth- and thirteenth-century temples at Belur, Halebid and Somnathpur. The Keshava temple at Somnathpur represents the climax of the development and is in many ways unique (Fig. 83). To begin with there are three sanctuaries dedicated to Vishnu in different forms, which open off a columned hall. The projections of the outer walls of the sanctuaries almost approach a circle in plan, or more precisely, a many-

84 Detail of the plinth of the Keshava temple, Somnathpur: the fine carving of mythical beasts, warriors and foliage is in the easily workable medium of chloritic schist

sided star created by a number of rotated squares. The pillared hall which links the sanctuaries extends eastwards into a porch. The whole scheme is elevated on a platform surrounding the temple, repeating the pattern of the outer projections. The enclosure walls of the complex are provided with minor shrines and an entrance gateway.

In its external elevation the Somnathpur temple presents the essential characteristics of the Hoyshala style. The base of the platform is carved with horizontal mouldings whose profiles are sharply angular. The plinth of the temple consists of a number of horizontal bands carved with friezes—elephants at the base, above which are horses, mythical beasts, geese, lotus designs and mythological and processional scenes (Fig. 84). The outer walls of the sanctuaries are furnished with carvings of images beneath trees; miniature ornamental superstructure designs function as surmounting pediments. The superstructures continue the projections of the walls beneath, and are divided into horizontal divisions which diminish as they ascend, capped with inverted-bell-like roof forms. At the front of each of the three superstructures is a projection housing important sacred icons. There are almost no solid walls to the hall and porch of the temple, which are enclosed by pierced stone screens filtering the light. The columns of the hall and porch reflect the decorative brilliance of the Hoyshala craftsmen; some columns were turned on a lathe to produce perfect circular sections, while others had their shafts fluted and moulded with a variety of decorative motifs. The overhanging brackets of the porch support an inclined eave above which rises the parapet.

The Later Chalukya style of temple building preserves its origins in the temple forms evolved under the patronage of the Early Chalukyas at Aihole and other sites, the superstructures, for example, being composed of a stepped series of eave mouldings. Examples of Later Chalukya temple architecture are found at such sites as Lakkundi, Gadag and Ittagi, belonging to the eleventh and twelfth centuries. Their architectural features embody to some extent a fossilized vocabulary of Early Chalukya features, but actually the Later Chalukya temples do not belong to the mainstream of southern stylistic development. Rather, it is the attention paid to the precise detailing of the architectural masses, with a particular regard for horizontal mouldings, that emerges as one of the key characteristics of this style. The superstructure itself is diminished in importance as the horizontal elevation of the temple becomes increasingly emphasized by extensive open porches and halls. In these parts of the temple it is the devices of balcony seating, carved columns and overhanging angled eaves that provide the principal external effect.

The southern style under the Vijayanagas and Nayakas (fifteenth to seventeenth centuries)

From the twelfth century onwards the south Indian temple continued to evolve under the patronage of the Pandya, Vijayanaga and Nayaka rulers. Its growth into a gigantic urban ensemble reflects the increasingly dominant role of the temple in city life particularly developed under the Vijayanaga empire in the fifteenth and sixteenth centuries. This growth continued up to the seventeenth century, after which a period of cultural decline set in due to the Muslim and European invasions. With the patronage of the rulers of the Vijayanaga empire, the most powerful and wealthy dynasty of south India, the principle of monumentalism as expressed in an expansion and repetition of architectural elements came greatly to influence the conception of the temple. Even though the sanctuary remained the most sacred part of the temple, great attention was paid to the outlying elements of the complex. Temple building was characterized by a desire to enlarge earlier sacred structures by the addition of successive enclosure walls, entered by a number of gateways (Fig. 85). The circuits thus created permit circumambulation

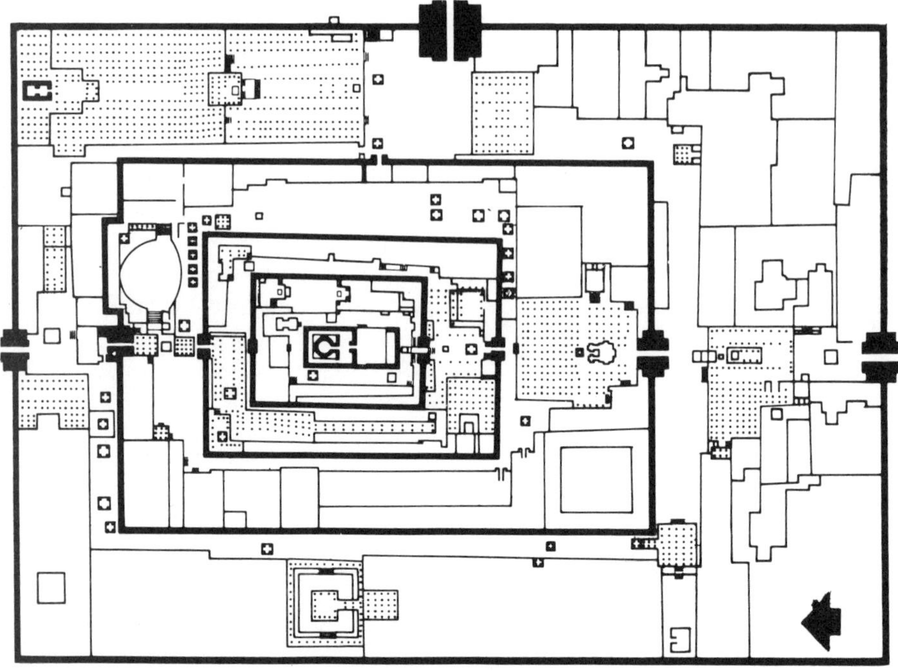

85 Plan of the Vishnu temple, Shrirangam. The original sanctuary is at the centre of the temple and is surrounded by concentric enclosures added at different periods

of the sanctuary and also link it to a number of additional structures in a harmonious ensemble. In fact, it became the custom to add to already existing temples rather than to erect new ones, reflecting the belief that sanctity cannot easily be transferred. In order to enlarge a temple a series of enclosure walls was added until the original sanctuary was surrounded by a number of expanding circuits, lending the temple the appearance of a walled fortress. These walls were mostly utilitarian structures sometimes provided with inner platforms and battlements as a means of defence in times of emergency.

The chief architectural feature of these walls is their towered gateways, or *gopuras*, whose origins are traced back to the early structures of the Pallavas. From the period of the Pandya rulers in the twelfth century these gateways emerge as a dominant element in the outer appearance of the temple (Fig. 86). *Gopuras* were raised at all cardinal points consistent with the expanding number of enclosure walls. As they were built to ever greater heights their structural ostentation came to overshadow the inner sanctuary, whose original superstructure was frequently lost to view. A typical *gopura* is rectangular in plan with a central opening at ground level provided with wooden doors, often decorated with brass fixtures. Above rises the tapering tower, usually with a slightly concave profile (Fig. 87). As on the walls and

86 Pampati temple, Vijayanagara, sixteenth century: the sanctuary within the enclosure walls is dwarfed by the soaring gateway towers (*gopuras*)

superstructure of the sanctuary itself, the tower of the *gopura* is divided into a number of storeys which repeat on a diminishing scale the features of the walls beneath. On the summit of the tower is the characteristic barrel vaulted roof form. These towers are celebrated for their rich ornamentation in which figural sculptures, executed in painted stucco and brick, are provided at each storey to give visible expression to the vast pantheon of Hindu gods and goddesses, their consorts and attendant figures (Fig. 88).

The impulse to develop gigantic temple complexes with prominent gateways reflects the changing role of the temple which, in the Vijayanaga period, became more closely involved with the life of the town; in fact, its expanding enclosures frequently extended into the town itself as, for example, at Shrirangam (Fig. 85). As temples grew they employed an increasing proportion of the community as ritual programmes became more and more

87 *Opposite* Gateway (*gopura*) and tank, Minakshi temple, Madurai, seventeenth century

88 *Above* Sculptures on one of the gateways, Minakshi temple, Madurai: the innumerable painted stucco figures represent the divine pantheon

complicated. It is associated functions of the temple, such as civic meetings, education, dance and theatre, that account for the innumerable columned halls and artificial tanks of water that were contained within temple walls, such as at Madurai and other towns. There were also additional pavilions for the consorts of the gods and their vehicles.

The overall stylistic principles of repetition and continuous expansion led to a general tendency to multiply the elements of the vertical profile of the walls; the plinth, for example, splits up into an ever greater number of elements, and the wall too is divided into further horizontal subdivisions by the application of intermediate mouldings. The greatest attention, however, was paid to matters of surface decoration, particularly of the columns which were employed throughout the halls and processional corridors of the temple complex. Under the Vijayanaga rulers the so-called 'thousand-pillared halls' first became popular, the columns being decorated with considerable skill and artistry. A striking example of pillar design, and indeed that most frequently used, transforms the shaft into a central core of carved statuary, often of monumental size and carved entirely in the round. One of the most characteristic themes, especially employed for the outer row of columns of the halls, displays a rearing horse or beast with rider supported by attendants or mythical animals (Fig. 89). The virtuosity of such carvings represents a high point in the evolution of craft traditions in south India. The brackets of these columns exhibit considerable complexity in their design, projecting outwards by means of extended figures, beasts or inverted lotus designs. Free-standing columns or *stambhas*, often of metal, were also utilized as supports for various sacred images.

By far the largest of the fully developed south Indian temples is that at Shrirangam (Fig. 85), built over many centuries but particularly expanded during the Vijayanaga period. An unusual feature of the plan is that it is laid out from north to south instead of the usual east–west orientation. The sanctuary is dedicated to Vishnu and dates from the Pandya period in the twelfth century. The dimensions of the temple reached by the Nayaka period in the seventeenth century are remarkable—the outermost wall is a rectangle of more than 850 by 750 metres. Contained within this area are six enclosure circuits with the shrine at the centre. The three outer courts extend through and into the surrounding town, their gateways rising above the roof-tops of the houses. Within the walls of the temple are numerous hypostyle halls, open colonnades and covered artificial tanks.

Temple styles of Bengal and Kerala (twelfth century to modern period)

The tropical heavy rainfall zones of Bengal and Kerala are characterized by their distinct local architectural styles which influenced the forms of sacred structures that were evolved in these regions. The brick temples of Bengal present a unique architectural development in which can be seen the

89 *Left* Colonnade within the Raghunatha temple, Shrirangam

90 Keshta Raya temple, Bishnupur, seventeenth century

influence of timber and bamboo techniques of construction. Especially typical of these temples is the sloping roof with a curved ridge and pot finials. Mostly dating from the seventeenth century onwards, the Bengal temples are modest in scale and illustrate a considerable variety of building types indicating an extensive improvisation within a local architectural idiom. The temples at Bishnupur, for example, are built with a variety of roof forms on square and rectangular plans. The Keshta Raya temple at this site (Fig. 90) dates from the middle of the seventeenth century and illustrates well the typical roof form rising above walls richly decorated with terracotta plaques. This temple consists of two rectangular structures united together, their double curved roofs supporting an elevated square chamber with a curved sloping roof. In other temples this characteristic curved ridged roof form is frequently treated as a movable element in the vertical elevation and is sometimes reduced in scale and placed above an open porch structure. In this way, superstructures often multiply into five or more elements arranged in ascending tiers.

Of chief interest in the Bengal temples are the terracotta tiles which are applied to the outer surfaces, especially to the spandrels above the arches and doorways. These tiles are carved with scenes from mythology as well as sacred images (Fig. 14), and their rich variety of motifs embodies the efforts of local craft traditions which had their origins in the decoration of brick buildings erected under Buddhist patronage more than a thousand years earlier. The Bengal temples were erected at a time when the major

91 Vadakkunnatha temple, Trichur, sixteenth or seventeenth century

part of northern India was under Muslim influence: thus they contain arches with typically Islamic contours and are built on plan types that probably owe their popularity to Muslim usage. Conversely, contemporary Mughal architecture makes use of the so-called 'Bengal roof', often reconstructed in sandstone or marble.

The temples of Kerala also form a distinct group and, like those from Bengal, are characterized by their unique roof systems. These usually consist of low and overhanging eaves which rise in a series of diminishing gables covered with tiles and supported on a wooden frame. The walls of the temples are stone, usually granite, providing a core to the timber superstructure. The Vadakkunnatha temple at Trichur (Fig. 91) was founded in the fifteenth or sixteenth century and the treatment of its outer walls attests to the influence of contemporary Vijayanaga architecture. Sloping roofs are arranged in three tiers with gables projecting on four sides from the uppermost roof.

The Kerala temples display considerable variety in their plan types and square, circular or apsidal-ended buildings are all utilized, often in combination with columned halls. The earliest examples in Kerala go back to the twelfth century and mostly consist of single structures; in later centuries there was the development of the temple complex in which the main sanctuary was hidden within a number of porches and minor shrines.

8 The Temples of South-East Asia

The stylistic origins of the Hindu temples of 'greater India' are still obscure, even though it is possible to trace some individual architectural and decorative elements from the ancient monuments of this region to various sources within India, both northern and southern. But no temple within India as a whole can be compared with the buildings erected under the Shailendra and Khmer dynasties in Java and Cambodia, for example. It is as if the architects of the temples of South-East Asia reassembled the stylistic elements that they had learnt about, but perhaps never seen, in accordance with theoretical prescriptions about temple building exported from India. There is always the impression that Hindu architecture outside India is more orthodox and conservative in its formal aspect. There is also a more concerted attempt to link architectural forms with cosmological and other beliefs. The same is also true of the Buddhist monuments of South-East Asia. Striking among the qualities of Hindu temples outside India is their ability to create an architectural layout that embodies elements of myth. The most spectacular example of this is seen in the great temple complexes at Angkor, devised to function as allegories of the creation myth of the churning of the cosmic ocean.

In the extensive and symmetrical ensembles of Hindu temples outside India, there is found a concentration on axial planning and strict orientation according to the cardinal directions. There is also the association of sacred architecture with the royal capital, to be distinguished from the south Indian city-temple. The identification of the ruler with a divinity permitted the Hindu temples of South-East Asia to function both as a place of the gods and as a memorial to the king, who was considered divinity in human form. This concept never truly gained popularity in India but had a considerable influence upon architectural developments in Java and Cambodia, where building projects of ever increasing magnitude expressed the temporal ambition of the ruler. It was probably this impulse that promoted the linking together of isolated structures into extensive architectural complexes such as those that were developed under Khmer patronage. Hindu temples of South-East Asia also embody another concept that rarely finds expression within India—the identification of the cosmic mountain Meru with the terraced temple.

Java

The earliest Hindu temples in Java were probably erected during the period of the Shailendra dynasty which held sway over central Java in the eighth and

92 Chandi Bhima, Dieng Plateau, Central Java, eighth century: the forms of this building are clearly Indian in origin

ninth centuries. Two groups of modest structures built of volcanic stone are found at the mountain sites of Dieng and Gdong Songo. The eight temples of the Dieng plateau are all dedicated to Shiva and possibly belong to the eighth century. They comprise single-celled shrines, with entrances on one side which in some examples are extended to create a small vestibule. The temples are elevated on deeply moulded plinths and the walls above are divided by shallow pilasters, with niches in the centres of each side. A clearly demarcated cornice delimits the wall height. Great attention is paid to the ornamentation of the wall niches and doorway, and here there is the earliest usage of the auspicious demonic mask and open-jawed aquatic monster that becomes such a characteristic feature of Javanese and Balinese art. In the superstructures of the Dieng temples a variety of Indian stylistic influences is to be detected: Chandi Arjuna employs the system of repeating the principal features of the main wall at a reduced scale so that a pyramid-like profile is achieved; in contrast, the tower of Chandi Bhima rises in a number of storeys with ribbed fruit motifs and arched 'windows' out of which faces peer (Fig. 92). The temples at Gdong Songo are of the same architectural scheme as those at Dieng, though there is an increased emphasis given to the mouldings of the plinth and cornice. Temple number 3 at Gdong Songo has a projecting vestibule forming the entrance to the sanctuary, flanked on either side by guardian figures; the lintel above is fashioned into a curved bow-like contour.

Most of the monuments of central Java that post-date these two groups are Buddhist and display a continuous evolution of architectural form and decoration. The last great building of the Shailendra period indicates the revival of Hinduism that was to mark the end of Buddhism in this region—this is the temple of Lara Jonggrang at Prambanan, erected in the late ninth or tenth century and dedicated to a trio of Hindu divinities (Fig. 93). The temple consists of a complex of principal shrines and minor sanctuaries incorporating no less than 232 structures. The plan is centred on a square

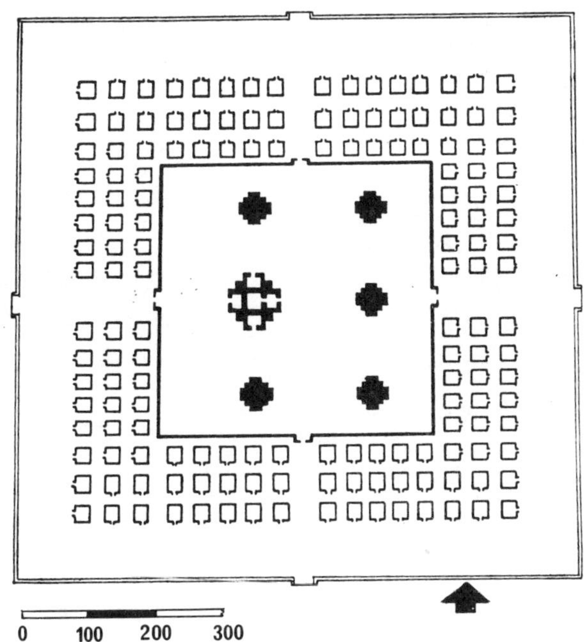

93 Plan of the Larajonggrang temple, Prambanan, Central Java, ninth or tenth century: the central Shiva shrine dominates the accessory structures

enclosure with three main shrines in a line, devoted to Vishnu, Brahma and Shiva; the latter deity is housed in the largest and central structure (Fig. 94). Facing these sanctuaries are three smaller shrines accommodating images of the animal or bird vehicle appropriate to each god. Outside the enclosure are minor shrines arranged in rows, now mostly ruined. The focus of the Prambanan ensemble is the Shiva shrine, which consists of a central chamber surrounded on three sides by subsidiary chambers housing images of Shiva, Ganesha and Durga; a vestibule forms the entrance to the principal shrine. Around these is an open ambulatory passageway with relief carvings illustrating scenes from the *Ramayana* (Fig. 7). The shrine is elevated on a high platform divided into panels and carved with protective motifs such as trees burdened with garlands, half-bird musicians, and auspicious females. At the terrace level rows of miniature shrines are surmounted by ribbed spherical elements with bell-like finials. The walls of the main shrine are divided into two registers by a horizontal moulding, and have recessed niches framed by demonic masks. Above a heavy cornice rises the superstructure in a series of diminishing storeys marked by ribbed spherical elements one of which functions as the crowning roof form. The numerous small shrines of this complex repeat the essential scheme of the Shiva temple.

In the tenth century the centre of political and cultural life in Java moved to the eastern parts of the island, and it is here that the next group of monuments is found. The earlier central Javanese temples are characterized by a strongly felt Indian influence, which governed both the overall conception of structural forms and many of the designs of carved decoration. However, in the eastern Javanese period, particularly from the thirteenth century onwards, a more localized idiom asserted itself and continued to develop into the modern period in the art of Bali.

Two monuments dating from the thirteenth century, a period when eastern Java was under the rule of the Singasari dynasty, give a clear idea of the evolved Javanese temple. Chandi Kidal consists of a square sanctuary raised on a platform which may have housed an image of Shiva, sometimes considered to be a post-mortem portrait of the local king Anushpati. The doorway and niches of the shrine are framed by demonic masks, and foliate decoration is applied to the walls. The east Javanese features are to be seen in the stepped overhanging mouldings of the plinth, cornice and lintels. Above rises the pyramidal superstructure. A simpler architectural scheme of the same basic type is found at Chandi Singasari.

Under the Majapahit dynasty from the fourteenth century onwards, the temple complex at Panataran was begun, possibly intended to enshrine the ashes of princes of the ruling dynasty. The Panataran ensemble is characterized by an irregularly laid out number of shrines, enclosure walls and gateways (Fig. 95); the structures themselves are quite small and repeat the architectural scheme epitomized in such earlier monuments as Chandi

94 *Left* Shiva shrine, Larajonggrang temple, Prambanan

Kidal. The tower has been reduced here to a number of horizontal mouldings which step back as they ascend, separated by deep recesses. Also to be found at Panataran are a number of terraces upon which wooden structures were probably erected. The bases of the shrines and plinths at Panataran are carved with narrative friezes depicting many Hindu legends.

The temples built during the Majapahit period at other sites in eastern Java are mostly in brick and consist of small isolated buildings. There is a tendency to prolong the upper portions of the structure, and the horizontal divisions are also emphasized. The preference for elevated platforms continues and these frequently have their bases carved with narrative reliefs. Chandi Surawana is typical of the series and dates from the end of the fourteenth century. It seems to have been erected for a member of the royal family and its purpose may have been linked with a funerary function.

Bali

Among the earliest of the monuments surviving in Bali is the royal bathing establishment at Goa Gadjah. This is related to similar sacred pools in Java belonging to the Singasari dynasty, from which a number of stone images of Hindu deities have been recovered. The Balinese example, probably contemporary with eleventh-century east Javanese buildings, has staircases leading down to an enclosed rectangular pool fed by natural springs. The spouts by which the water enters the pool are fashioned into sculptures of auspicious females holding pots. Overlooking the bath is a natural cave which functions as a temple, its outer face carved in the semblance of a demonic mask.

The rock-cut temple façades at Tampaksiring, known as Gunung Kawi, date from the same period as the bath at Goa Gadjah. Holes in their bases housed caskets which were probably meant to contain the ashes of the local rulers. The elevations of these rock-cut temples display the features familiar from contemporary east Javanese temples—the boldly moulded base and overhanging cornice, together with the tiered and diminishing superstructure composed of miniature elements. A false doorway interrupts the plinth and cornice.

Almost all the Hindu temples of Bali are constructed of brick with carved stone lintels and cornices. The superstructures are often built entirely of timber and rise in a series of thatched sloping roofs which diminish as they ascend. Most temples date only from the modern period, owing to the frequent earthquakes that beset the island. An essential part of every Balinese temple is the enclosure wall, entered by a prominent brick gateway which reproduces the characteristic features of Javanese architecture from

95 *Opposite* Shiva shrine, Panataran, Eastern Java, fourteenth century
96 *Overleaf left* Gateway to a modern temple, Bali
97 *Overleaf right* Priest officiating at the 'mother' temple, Besakih, Bali, which faces the volcano Gunung Agung: the tiers of the superstructures are thatched

the Majapahit period (Fig. 96). There is usually no lintel, the gateway presenting the appearance of a façade that has been split apart. Inside the enclosure are a number of small temples housing the various divinities, ranging from household and local deities to the cult gods and goddesses of Indian Hinduism. Each shrine consists of a simple sanctuary in brick or timber approached by a flight of steps; above rises the superstructure, known in Bali as 'Meru'.

The great 'mother' temple of Besakih probably dates from as early as the fourteenth century and is orientated towards the principal volcano of the island, Gunung Agung, considered to be the centre of the Balinese cosmography (Fig. 97). The temple is arranged in a number of ascending courtyards linked by long flights of stairs and stepped terraces. The sequence of split brick gateways and thatched 'Merus' is aligned on a single axis which leads the devotee ever upwards and nearer to the sacred mountain to which the temple is dedicated.

Balinese Hindu art is still evolving today, and largely concentrates on the decoration of sacred architecture. Sculpture is executed in soft volcanic stone or timber set into brick walls. The disintegration of forms into foliation remains a striking stylistic feature of Balinese art, which is primarily concerned with the depiction of the demonic. Masks and fierce guardian figures are constantly required to provide essential protection for the many temples of the island.

Cambodia

The earliest of the Indianized Cambodian kingdoms, Funan, was situated on the delta of the Mekong river and by the fourth century this empire was firmly established. Traces of brick structures have been found from this period, evidently intended to house stone sculptures of Hindu deities. In the seventh century political rule of the area shifted to the state of Chen La and it is from this period that the earliest Hindu temples in Cambodia survive. The principal Chen La temples are found at Sambor Prei Kuk. Temple 17 from the northern group at this site is a simple stone structure which imitates many of the features of contemporary Indian temples—moulded plinth, pilastered wall, carved lintel and flat roof; even the characteristic miniature arched 'windows' are found applied to the mouldings. More elaborate are the two temples numbers 7 and 22, also from the northern group at Sambor Prei Kuk, in which brick is combined with carved stone for the pilasters and lintels of the doorways. These temples are square or octagonal in plan, but their outer elevations are essentially the same. The walls are raised on a moulded plinth and are provided with projecting niches in which sculptural compositions are carved. The superstructures rise in a series of stepped eave-like mouldings separated by recesses. Temple 1 from the southern group at the same site is the most evolved of the group and introduces pronounced projections in the centre of each side, carried up into the superstructure. Of interest in the temples at Sambor Prei Kuk are the corbelled techniques of

98 Prah Koh, Roluos, Cambodia, ninth century

creating the superstructures and the delicate foliate ornament executed in stucco on brick. From this period a number of carved stone lintels survive, which employ the characteristic Indian formula of garlands with jewels and tassels suspended between two open-jawed aquatic monsters upon whom ride *ganas*.

Towards the end of the eighth century the state of Chen La disintegrated, to be succeeded by the long-lived Khmer empire. The royal personality linked with the establishment of the Khmer dynasty is the ruler Jayavarman II who returned to Cambodia from Java to reunite the country. Following the progress of his conquests Jayavarman founded several capitals, finally settling on the Koulen plateau, north-east of Angkor. Here, according to Cambodian and Javanese custom, he carved an inscription describing himself as 'King of the Mountain'. Behind this sentiment was the belief in the sacredness of mountains on whose summits dwelt divinities related to the rulers of the country. Like the Hindu monuments of Java those of Cambodia were intended to convey the image of the sacred mountain. Jayavarman also established the royal cult which was to be such a feature of the religious life of the empire, and at the opening of the ninth century he erected a stone *linga* at Koulen, dedicating it to Shiva and assuming the royal title which invested him with divine power. The remains of the temple at Koulen display evidence of the new Khmer architectural style—especially the octagonal pilasters and carved lintel framing the doorways.

It was under the patronage of the late ninth-century king Indravarman that the first great works of Khmer sacred architecture were constructed. These buildings clearly defined the characteristic Khmer conception of a temple as a complex of small structures unified by axial planning. The symmetry of the parts was rigidly pursued, but was always combined with a strong sense of spatial sequence concentrating on the major east-west access by which these buildings were approached. The Prah Koh temple at Roluos (Fig. 98) is a funerary monument erected by Indravarman in memory of his royal ancestors. It comprises six detached sanctuaries dedicated to Shiva and his consort, identified with the male and female members of the royal family. These are elevated on a terrace and surrounded by enclosure walls in which accessory buildings, moats and gateways are incorporated. The sanctuaries are small square structures with a doorway in the centre of each side created by decorated pilasters supporting a carved lintel; only one doorway, however, actually provides access to the shrine, the others being false. The walls have a moulded plinth and overhanging cornice and there are also guardian figures. The superstructure is divided into a number of stepped and diminishing storeys repeating the scheme of the plinth, wall and cornice.

Also built by Indravarman is the Bakong temple at Roluos which was intended to be the ruler's own *lingam* shrine on top of a sacred mountain (Fig. 99). At the centre of this complex are five square and ascending terraces, approached by staircases in the centre of each side. At the summit is a single shrine with an elongated superstructure. One characteristic Khmer

99 Bakong, Roluos, ninth century

100 *Left* Baksei Chamkrong, Angkor, Cambodia, tenth century
101 *Above* Pre Rup, Angkor, tenth century

stylistic feature is already fully developed here: the sanctuary is provided with flame-like motifs which terminate each level of the tower. This sandstone terrace and shrine system, itself a complete temple-mountain, is enclosed by walls in which minor shrines, long galleries and gateways are placed. Associated with the Bakong temple are a series of portrait sculptures

102 Doorway, Banteay Srei temple, Angkor, tenth century

of Indravarman and his wives, as well as sacred images of Shiva, the patron deity of the king.

To Indravarman is attributed the founding of the city of Angkor, the royal capital of the Khmer empire. The great technological achievement associated with this city is the elaborate irrigation scheme which was laid out under Indravarman and continuously enlarged by his successors. It employed a number of gigantic artificial reservoirs called *barays* which were linked together by rectangular grids of canals. From these spread out a vast system of channels to water the rice paddies whose produce provided the economic basis for the Khmer empire.

The first great monument to be erected at Angkor was the temple-mountain of Bakheng, built by Yashovarman towards the end of the ninth century. This temple was constructed upon a natural hill and functioned as the sacred centre of the city, surrounded on four sides by moats and enclosure walls. The Bakheng temple has five terraces connected by axial flights of steps flanked by guardian lions and provided with miniature shrines. The uppermost level has four corner shrines around a central one, representing the five peaks of Meru. A number of small buildings cluster around the base. Simpler temple-mountain schemes were also built at this period, such as the Baksei Chamkrong (Fig. 100), but not until the middle of the tenth century were these specifically identified with the divine spirit of the king. Pre Rup probably represents the first temple at Angkor to function as a permanent shrine for a ruler; it repeats many of the features of the earlier Bakheng temple, to which it adds the long galleries characteristic of the evolved Khmer style (Fig. 101).

The temple of Banteay Srei represents one of the finest achievements of the Khmer artistic tradition. It was built in the middle of the tenth century by a private individual in the court of Jayavarman V, and judging by the sophistication of this ensemble he was evidently a man of great taste. The temple comprises three small shrines arranged in a row and elevated upon a terrace surrounded by concentric enclosures and gateways. On the terraces are groups of free-standing mythical guardian figures (Fig. 13), some of which are also reproduced at either side of the doorways to the shrines. Pink sandstone is employed throughout. Of great interest in the architecture of this ensemble is the attention paid to the pediments; those over the gateways are triangular compositions clearly suggestive of timber construction, with 'beams' which meet in a gable-like fashion, but over the shrine doorways the pediments introduce curved wavy bands of foliations framing mythological scenes (Fig. 102). Also found at Banteay Srei is the quasi-vaulted roof in which corbelled stone courses reproduce the effect of a tiled roof on curved timbers, and windows with turned 'bars' of stone, which light the gateways and galleries.

Throughout the Banteay Srei complex there is a prolific use of delicately carved foliate decoration applied in bands to the plinth, pilasters and cornice of the walls. On the lintels the carving becomes deeper and figurative, and animal elements are introduced into the foliation. For the superstructures the foliation becomes almost three-dimensional, taking on a flame-like appearance, sometimes in combination with multi-serpent hoods and Garuda figures. There is also a particular decorative treatment of the false entrances, which are carved in semblance of timber doors complete with central post and side jambs.

The development of Khmer architecture over the following three centuries reveals the desire on the part of royal patrons to increase the scale of their building projects into ever more complicated and impressive architectural ensembles. Terraced schemes are combined with concentric enclosures, and there is a tendency to link together isolated structures with long colonnades. There is also a preference for rectangular plans, slightly elongated in an east-west direction. The masterpiece of Khmer architecture belongs to the twelfth century—this is the celebrated Angkor Vat built by Suryavarman II and dedicated to Vishnu (Figs 103–104). This great complex of shrines, corridors, gateways and enclosure walls covers an area in excess of 400 by 300 metres and is executed throughout in grey-black sandstone. The temple is orientated towards the west instead of the more usual direction of east, and there is also the unusual device of having the narrative panels of the outer colonnades arranged in an anticlockwise direction. These reversals of the usually strictly observed orientational systems employed throughout Hindu architecture, and especially at Angkor, indicate the special function of this building as a temple of the underworld—Angkor Vat is, in fact, a mortuary temple for Suryavarman. This is borne out by the subject of the sculptural friezes of the temple, some of which depict the life of the king; Yama, the god of death, also appears prominently.

The central part of Angkor Vat consists of an elevated complex of five shrines approached by steep flights of steps and linked together by colonnades. This central part is surrounded by two concentric colonnades at lower levels with corner shrines and gateways aligned with the central shrine. The towers that surmount these shrines and gateways are of the standard Khmer form and are skilfully combined into a dramatic external elevation, of which the climax is the uppermost central shrine. The temple is approached by an extended platform and road flanked by a balustrade fashioned into the body of a serpent. The temple is surrounded by a moat, the access road becoming a bridge. Thus is suggested a recreation of the Hindu cosmological system, in which Meru forms the focal point for the concentrically arranged continents and oceans.

The extensively sculptural compositions with which Angkor Vat is furnished are mostly located along the inner walls of the semi-enclosed colonnades. Here are found scenes from the *Mahabharata*, the life of the founder king, and images of various Hindu deities. Including numerous representations of the *apsarases*, the celestial consorts of the gods, the art of the temple is intended to suggest the heavenly paradise of the god-king (Fig. 10).

At the opening of the thirteenth century, the city of Angkor Thom was laid out by Jayavarman VII. Its surrounding walls and moats form part of a

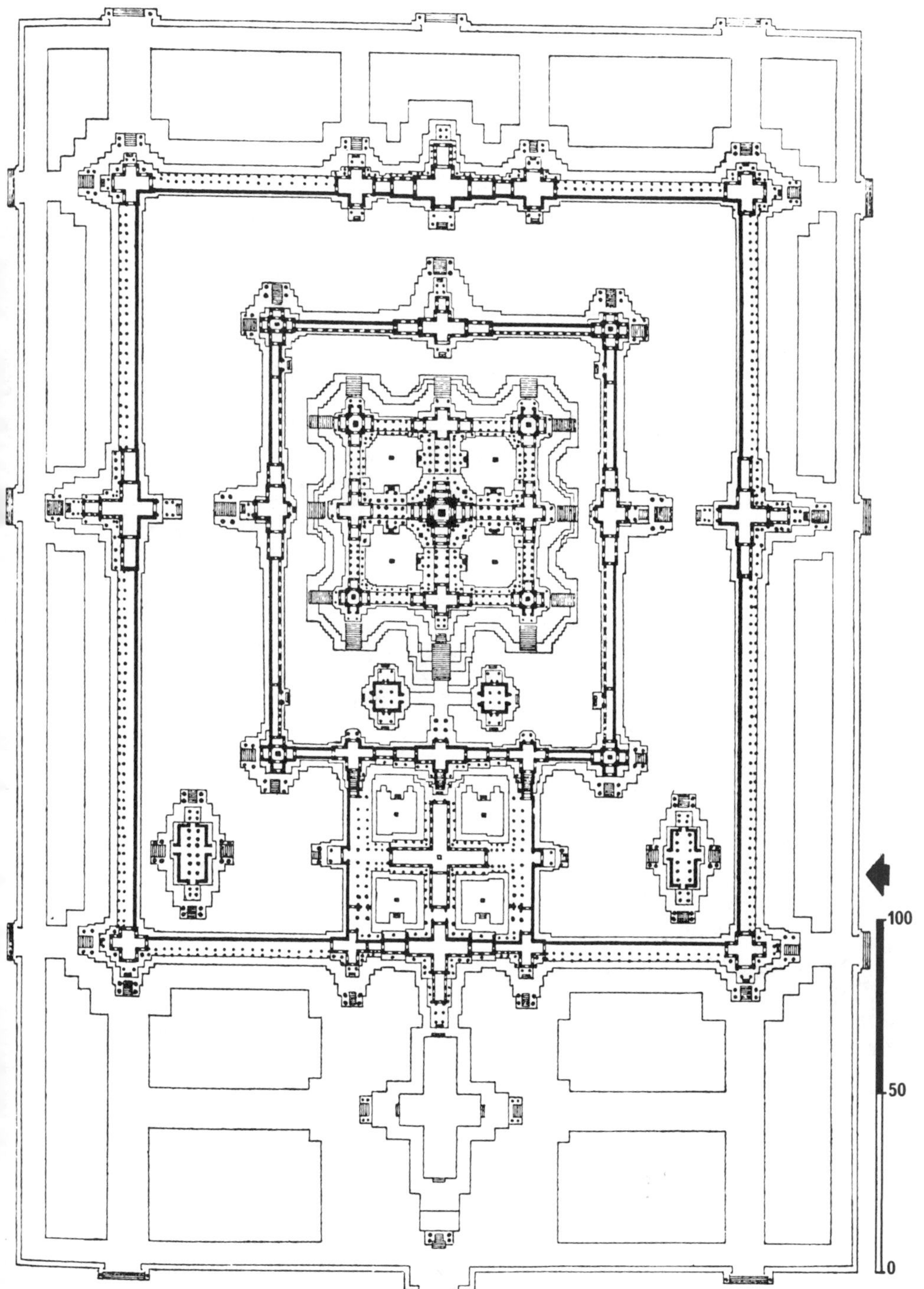

103 Central complex of Angkor Vat, twelfth century: a number of concentric courtyards on ascending levels lead towards the central shrine

104 Approach to Angkor Vat

gigantic square, some four kilometres long on each side. These walls are provided with monumental gateways surmounted by towers carved in the semblance of the face of the king looking out in four directions. The precise meaning of these heads is not clear but they may be taken to indicate the power of the king radiating outwards. Elephants lift lotus flowers in their trunks and flank the entrances, whose approaches are defined by long serpent balustrades held on one side of the road by gods, and by demons on the other side, in illustration of the myth of the churning of the cosmic ocean (Fig. 2). The focal point of Angkor Thom is the temple of the Bayon in which Mahayana Buddhism is introduced, mingled with ancestor cults. The Buddhist phase was not to last long and after the death of Jayavarman VII Angkor rapidly declined, marking the end of Hinduism in Cambodia.

Vietnam

From the sixth century the southern part of what is now Vietnam constituted the important kingdom of Champa. The history of this empire was mostly troubled, owing to the frequent devastation of the country by Javanese, Khmer and Chinese invaders. Although the Cham rulers were never to achieve the great concentration of wealth characteristic of the Khmer kings, they subscribed to the cult of divine kingship and were concerned with the post-mortem deification of royal individuals. The groups of temples at their various capitals functioned as sanctuaries in which the divine was 'personalized'.

Cham temple architecture seems to have followed its course of evolution alongside that of the Khmers, but Cham architects never attempted to link architectural elements together in order to create symmetrical temple complexes. Temple sites of the Cham country consist of irregularly laid out groups of isolated structures. The earliest temples that have survived in Vietnam date from the tenth and eleventh centuries and are found at the sites of Mi Son, Hoa Lai (Fig. 105), Dong Duong and Po Nagar. These temples are all of the same basic scheme—a square brick structure consisting of a sanctuary with projecting doorways on all four sides. Only that to the west actually provides access to the interior of the shrine, and is prominently displayed. At the base of the elevation of the temple is a moulded plinth upon which the wall rises, divided into vertical projections and recesses by bands of foliate ornament. Characteristic of these early Cham temples are the doorways which are provided with double pediments, one contained within the other, or one surmounting the other, created by curved and wavy foliage bands. Flame-like motifs, known from Khmer monuments, are also found in which foliation and serpent bodies are combined. The wall is terminated by a stepped overhanging cornice above which rises the superstructure. This is composed of a series of stepped storeys which diminish as they ascend. Unfortunately, many of these buildings have their uppermost portions badly ruined. One feature of these temples which distinguishes

105 North tower, Hoa Lai, Vietnam, eleventh century

them from contemporary Khmer architecture is the provision of a pedestal within the sanctuary to hold free-standing sacred images.

The history of the Hindu temple architecture of Vietnam may be viewed as an improvisation with a single temple model. In later temples, such as those at Bin Dinh which date from the twelfth century, certain developments are to be found: the entrance to the sanctuary is extended to create a small vestibule and the superstructure is provided with miniature curved roof forms, not unlike northern Indian styled towers, which are positioned at each level. After the Mongol invasion in the later thirteenth century, the impulse of Hindu temple building in Vietnam was interrupted; thereafter, Buddhism was to become increasingly pervasive in the area.

9 The Hindu Temple Today

Hinduism remains a vibrant cultural and religious force in India, the sub-Himalayan valleys, and Bali, where new temples continue to be erected and older buildings refurbished. No village in Hindu Asia is complete without a temple to house the sacred images of cult gods and goddesses as well as various local deities and protective divinities essential for the happiness and success of the community. Sometimes these temples are located in the vicinity of more elaborate but older buildings whose sanctity is now lost. Temples currently in worship are recognized by their whitewashed surfaces, and fluttering flags which signify that the deity is 'in residence'.

In India the categories of 'northern' and 'southern' may still be applied to sacred building activity. In the south of India there has been no distinct break in architectural traditions, and modern temples are built in a style that is a direct continuation of that perfected under Vijayanaga and Nayaka patronage. Temple building in the north is the product of a more discontinuous tradition, but temples still follow the forms developed during the period of the Chandellas, Kalingas and Solankis.

Since the period of the most ambitious temple building activities—the eleventh and twelfth centuries in the north of India, and the fifteenth and sixteenth centuries in the south—there has been a tendency to repeat well-formulated architectural models, in accordance with the inherently conservative character of Hindu art and culture. However, temple projects in later centuries were mostly reduced in scale when much of the country came under foreign rule and economic wealth was no longer exclusively in the hands of Hindu rulers. An inevitable decline in building patronage and artistic traditions has occurred in India, and craft traditions are dying out. There are fewer and fewer skilled masons and carvers to execute the images and decorative motifs that once adorned the outer surfaces and interior halls of temples. New materials such as concrete and steel have appeared, and these to some extent now replace the more costly and cumbersome stone or brick, though there is little evidence that these materials have influenced the overall conception of temple form. Thus concrete is moulded to reproduce the curved and clustered towers typical of the central northern Indian temple. At one of the most ambitious modern temple projects now being undertaken in India, the reconstruction of the Shiva temple at Somnath in Gujarat, cement is employed as a refinement to stone carving. Dating back to the twelfth century and destroyed by Muslim raiders, this temple has now been almost completely recreated in its original style, and sculptors are busily engaged in carving the final images for the outer walls and inner columns of the temple.

106 The minimal temple—*lingam* sheltered by sticks and leaves, overlooking the Malprabaha river, near Aihole

In the peripheral areas of Nepal, Bengal and Kerala a local architectural idiom has flourished in recent centuries, supported by a vigorous folk art. This is also true of Bali today. In these parts of Hindu Asia local master architects and craftsmen have ensured that temple styles continue their evolution. In Bali the carving of the soft volcanic stone with which temples are decorated is carried on, a particular feature being the elaboration of demonic themes.

As Western influences make themselves felt in the urban centres of Hindu Asia, it is in the small temples of village India, Nepal and Bali that the continuity of Hindu culture and architecture is best found today. Besides full-scale temples, isolated images or symbols of divinities, perhaps simply sheltered by sticks and leaves (Fig. 106), indicate that Hinduism is a living tradition for which even the most rudimentary of building forms may be appropriate. Man is still able to achieve contact with the world of the gods.

Further Reading

The list of suggested volumes is mostly restricted to general works; only the most recent publication date is given. Detailed bibliographies are included in almost all of these works.

Part One: The Meaning of the Temple

Banerjea, Jitendra Nath, *The Development of Hindu Iconography,* Calcutta: University of Calcutta, 1956.

Basham, A. L., *The Wonder that was India,* New York: Grove Press, 1959.

Boner, Alice, and Sharma, S. R., 'Economic and organizational aspects of the building operations of the Sun temple at Konarka', *Journal of the Economic and Social History of the Orient,* XIII, 3, Leiden, 1970.

Chaudhuri, Nirad, *Hinduism: A Religion to Live By,* New Delhi: B. I. Publications, 1979.

Danielou, Alain, *Hindu Polytheism,* London: Routledge & Kegan Paul, 1964.

de Barry, William, ed., *Sources of Indian Tradition,* New York: Columbia University Press, 1958 (original sources in translation).

Diehl, Carl, *Instrument and Purpose: Studies in Rites and Rituals in South India,* Lund: C. W. K. Gleerup, 1956.

Dowson, John, *A Classical Dictionary of Hindu Mythology and Religion, Geography, History and Literature,* Calcutta: Rupa & Co., 1982.

Eck, Diana L., *Darsan: Seeing the Divine Image in India,* 2d. ed., Chamberburg: Anima Books, 1985.

Galey, Jean-Claude, ed., *L'Espace du Temple,* 2 vols., Paris: Éditions de l'École des Hautes Études en Sciences Sociales (*Purusartha,* 8 and 10), 1985.

Gonda, Jan, *Visnuism and Sivaism: A Comparison,* London: Athlone, 1970.

Kulke, Hermann, and Rothermund, Dietmar, *A History of India,* New Delhi: Manchar Publications, 1986.

Lannoy, Richard, *The Speaking Tree: A Study of Indian Culture and Society,* Oxford: Oxford University Press, 1971.

O'Flaherty, Wendy, *Hindu Myths: A Sourcebook Translated from the Sanskrit,* London: Penguin Books, 1975.

Stein, Burton, ed., *South Indian Temples: An Analytical Reconsideration,* New Delhi: Vikas, 1978.

Stutely, Margaret, and Stutely, James, *A Dictionary of Hinduism: Its Mythology, Folklore and Development 1500 BC–AD 1500,* New Delhi, Heritage Publishers, 1986.

Zimmer, Heinrich, *Myths and Symbols in Indian Art and Civilization,* New York: Harper and Brothers, 1962.

Part Two: The Forms of the Temple

Acharya, Prasanna Kumar, *A Dictionary of Hindu Architecture,* New Delhi: Oriental Book Reprint, 1981.

Brown, Percy, *Indian Architecture (Buddhist and Hindu Periods),* Bombay: D. B. Taraporevala, 1976.

Dumarçay, Jacques, *The Temples of Java,* Singapore, 1986.

Frédéric, Louis, *The Temples and Sculpture of Southeast Asia,* London: Thames and Hudson, 1965.

Giteau, Madelaine, *The Civilization of Angkor,* New York: Rizzoli, 1976.

Harle, J. C., *The Art and Architecture of the Indian Subcontinent,* London: Penguin Books, 1986.

Huntington, Susan L., and Huntington, John C., *The Art of Ancient India,* New York and Tokyo: Weatherhill, 1985.

Kempers, A. J. Bernet, *Ancient Indonesian Art,* Amsterdam: C. P. J. Van Der Peet, 1959.

Kramrisch, Stella, *The Hindu Temple,* Delhi and Varanasi: Motilal Banarsidass, 1980.

Krishna, Deva, *Temples of North India,* New Delhi: National Book Trust, 1969.

Meister, Michael, and Dhaky, M. A., eds., *Encyclopaedia of Indian Temple Architecture,* Philadelphia: University of Pennsylvania Press; Delhi: Oxford University Press, 1983 (ongoing).

Michell, George, *The Penguin Guide to the Monuments of India,* Vol. 1: *Buddhist, Jain, Hindu,* London: Penguin Books, 1989.

Sivaramamurti, Calambur, *The Art of India,* New York: Harry N. Abrams, 1977.

Soundara Rajan, K. V., *Indian Temple Styles,* New Delhi: Munshiram Manoharlal, 1972.

Srinivasan, K. R., *Temples of South India,* New Delhi: National Book Trust, 1971.

Volwahsen, Andreas, *Living Architecture: India,* London: Macdonald, 1970.

Wiesner, Ulrich, *Nepalese Temple Architecture,* Leiden: E. J. Brill, 1978.

Indexes

Page numbers in italics denote illustrations

General Index

Index of Temple Sites

Asuras are demons
Not i'mean - eternal struggle
No ultimate resolution of g[illegible] evil